DISAPPOINTED
GUESTS

DISAPPOINTED GUESTS

Essays by
AFRICAN, ASIAN, AND
WEST INDIAN STUDENTS

Edited by
HENRI TAJFEL, M.A., Ph.D.
*University Lecturer in Social Psychology and
Fellow of Linacre House, Oxford*

and

JOHN L. DAWSON, M.A., D. Phil.
*Research Lecturer, Department of Social
Anthropology, University of Edinburgh*

*Issued under the Auspices of the
Institute of Race Relations, London*
OXFORD UNIVERSITY PRESS
LONDON   NEW YORK
1965

Oxford University Press, Amen House, London E.C.4

GLASGOW   NEW YORK   TORONTO   MELBOURNE   WELLINGTON
BOMBAY   CALCUTTA   MADRAS   KARACHI   LAHORE   DACCA
CAPE TOWN   SALISBURY   NAIROBI   IBADAN   ACCRA
KUALA LUMPUR   HONG KONG

Printed in Great Britain by the Camelot Press Ltd.
London and Southampton

Contents

Acknowledgements

We are grateful to the Institute of Race Relations for making the publication of this book possible. We are particularly indebted to Mr. Christopher Hill of the Institute for his help in organizing the competition and in preparing the final draft of the book. Dr. Bryan Wilson read the MS. of our own chapter. We are grateful for his comments and suggestions. The members of the jury for the competition whose names will be found in the Preface did an inordinate amount of work reading a large number of essays; we are grateful for their advice concerning the final selection for publication.

H. T.
J. L. D.

Preface

In the summer of 1963 the Institute of Race Relations agreed to sponsor an essay competition for African, Asian, and West Indian students. At the beginning of the academic year posters announcing the competition were displayed in colleges and universities throughout the country. They read as follows:

African, Asian and West Indian students who are reading for a first or higher Degree or for a Diploma at Universities, Colleges of Technology, Teacher Training Colleges and similar institutions in Britain are invited to take part in an Essay Competition. The essay should be on the general subject of the writer's attitudes towards the colour problem before he came to this country and the changes in these attitudes, if any, that may have occurred as a result of having spent some time in Britain. Competitors are free to base their essays on personal experience, to deal with the problem in general terms or to combine the two approaches.

The best essay was to be awarded a prize of £100. A jury, which comprised, in addition to the editors, Mr. George Bennett, Fellow of Linacre House and Senior Lecturer in Commonwealth History, Oxford, Professor Gustav Jahoda from the University of Strathclyde, and Mrs. Sheila Kitzinger, awarded the prize to Mr. Mervyn E. Morris of Jamaica. This book is a collection of essays chosen for publication from those which were received.

A book of essays drawn from the personal experiences of its authors would normally seek acceptance as a work of literary merit. A book on race relations, on the other hand, would usually be published as the result of a scientific study. This book cannot make either of these claims. If it does present evidence, it is rather in the sense of informal *témoignage*. The essays are not answers to a questionnaire distributed to a representative population of overseas students in Britain; those published in this book were not chosen on the basis of representativeness of the opinions

expressed, experiences described, countries of origin, universities, or subjects studied. We used fairly general criteria of
originality, intrinsic interest, liveliness or readability.

Nevertheless we believe that some sort of a coherent image
emerges, and that the unpremeditated unity of themes and the
core of agreement between people from so many different backgrounds cannot fail to impress. There are two characteristics that
all our authors share: they all came from abroad to study in this
country; and they are all coloured. These two characteristics
seem to determine a common experience of bitterness and disappointment. How much of it is due to colour and how much to
a clash of cultural backgrounds? Different views about this are
expressed in various essays; but it seems that the weight of
opinion is towards the first alternative.

The potential consequences of this are perhaps best expressed
in the words of a student from Nigeria who wrote in his essay:
'Down the ages, it has been the traveller who has helped to
disseminate knowledge and who served as the unofficial ambassador of his own country. And when this messenger of peace
is himself a student or a learner, the problem becomes more
threatening, as impressions of scholastic days are erased only
with difficulty, and most of the students of today are the leaders
of tomorrow in their respective countries.'

*   *   *

The essays which follow will translate into direct and personal
terms certain generalizations which we have attempted to sketch
out in the Epilogue. We feel that our comments cannot possibly
do justice to so many strongly felt and sincerely written reports
of personal experiences; we also feel that attention must be paid
to these reports by anyone who cares about the image of this
country abroad, and about men and women who came here to
learn and hope to go back as more useful citizens of their own
countries and of the world. It would be arrogant of us to express
in conclusion the customary few words of gratitude to the
students who wrote the essays and made this book possible. If the
book proves of any value at all, it will be because of teaching

others what we have already learnt from reading the essays. And we feel that ultimately its purpose is not just to help in reducing prejudice or discrimination, and thus to ease the path of one group of students in this country, important as those ends are. Perhaps the most significant lesson to be drawn from these essays is this simple conclusion: today no country can afford to forget that it cannot live alone.

HENRI TAJFEL
Oxford
JOHN L. DAWSON
Edinburgh

Feeling, Affection, Respect

MERVYN MORRIS

Jamaica

Mervyn E. Morris writes: 'I was born on February 21, 1937 in
Kingston, Jamaica. My father (who died in 1948) was an accoun-
tant in the Goverment service, my mother (who has now retired)
a school-teacher. After prep. and elementary schools I won a full
scholarship to Munro College (a boarding-school more or less
modelled on English public schools) which I attended from 1948
until 1954. I won a Jamaica Government Exhibition to the
University College of the West Indies where from 1954 until
1957 I read English, French, and History for a B.A. General
degree. (The UCWI, in special relation to the University of
London, taught for London University degrees.) I debated
regularly for the college and was Features Editor of the undergraduate magazine, *The Pelican*. I played lawn-tennis for Jamaica.
After graduating from UCWI I returned to Munro College to
teach. Awarded a Rhodes Scholarship, I entered St. Edmund Hall,
Oxford, in 1958. I won a lawn-tennis blue in 1959, 1960 and 1961
and got a Second in English. While at Oxford I wrote and read
radio essays for the B.B.C. Caribbean Service who also broadcast a few of my poems.

I returned home in 1961 to be an Assistant Registrar at UCWI
and to get married. I dislike full-time administration and left the
University of the West Indies (as UCWI had become) after a
year, to return to Munro College as Senior English Master. My
wife, who is a UCWI graduate, is Senior Spanish Teacher at
Munro. We have one son.

I write poems. I am a regular contributor to *Bim* (the "little
magazine" for which nearly all West Indian writers have at some
time written) and to *The Sunday Gleaner*. I contributed to the

Independence Anthology of Jamaican Literature and three poems by
me are to be published later this year in an anthology of Caribbean
literature edited by G. R. Coulthard for the University of London
Press. I have had poems, book reviews, and articles published
also in *Public Opinion, Caribbean Quarterly* (published by UWI)
and *The Times Literary Supplement*. I have written and broadcast
for the Jamaica Broadcasting Corporation.

I enjoy schoolmastering. Much of the work I have to do is
relevant to writing. I still enjoy playing games and helping with
debating, drama, and other school activities.

My keenest ambition is to write well and successfully. My
immediate aim is to get more poems accepted by magazines of
international standing and then to try and get a book of my
poems published.'

I HAVE been asked to write about my difficulties in Britain, about
anything that seemed connected with my reaction, as a West
Indian student, to Britain. As there are many books which can
give anyone who cares to read them a scientific view of the
racial situation in Britain, I have interpreted this undefined
request as an invitation to be personal, though I shall try to be
honest and, so far as possible, objective. When I have finished, it
should be fairly clear how at least one foreign student reacted to
Britain. What may seem contradictions I hope will be regarded as
complexities and ambiguities of which I have sometimes been
aware.

I found on arriving in England that to the English I was
primarily a foreigner distinguishable by my skin. There are
thousands of Blacks born in Britain, but (accurately enough)
everyone assumed I was a foreigner. Some of the men in my
college seemed surprised that I was familiar with their social
usages. I met the spontaneous friendliness for which St. Edmund
Hall has a well deserved reputation; here and there, perhaps, I
recognized an element of patronage or special concern to speak
to the black man but this was usually mingled with elements more
acceptable, such as honest curiosity. It was not an easy time for
any white Englishman to speak naturally to a Black, as the

Notting Hill riots, a few months before my arrival in England, had been followed by public discussion of race and racial problems, which, though necessary and helpful, produced self-consciousness in any racial situation.

Some of the ignorance I encountered I had been led to expect. Throughout England, and even in Oxford, I was told 'You speak English very well', and had to explain that English happened to be my native language. (A West Indian friend of mine once told a hyper-sophisticated cocktail-woman rather brusquely, 'You don't speak it so badly yourself!') I myself have never seriously been asked whether in the West Indies we live in trees, but I have been asked, in all solemnity, how many wives I had at home. The occasion was an interesting one in that there was no offence meant and none taken; the questioner genuinely wanted information.

I do not mind curiosity when it is genuine; for curiosity leads to inquiry and inquiry to information and information to understanding. Patronage, however, assumes information which proves the need to patronize; patronage is curious only to find those facts which seem to support the assumed position of superiority.

Children in homes I visited were often curious; the questions they asked were usually fundamental and innocent. Why was one side of my hand dark and the other light? They wanted to touch my hair. Why was my hair different from theirs?

Questions, and remarks, vary greatly in effect according to context. I was not often offended to hear friends use without thinking phrases harking back to slavery, such as 'working like a Black' and 'nigger in the woodpile'. It was often interesting to note which ones were sensitive enough to realize what they had said and how they then reacted. What mattered most to me usually was what seemed the intention of a remark, not the surface of the remark itself. It is possible to be more offensive asking with apparent politeness, 'How do you like it in England?' than asking frankly, 'How many wives do you have at home?'

Objective criteria on this sort of offensiveness are very difficult, probably impossible, to arrive at. It is like this with most prejudice in England, I gather, from my own experience, from my friends, and from what I have read. Ruth Glass in *The Newcomers*, which seems to me very accurate about the attitudes of West Indians in England, talks a great deal about the treacherous ambiguity of the racial situation. As George Mikes put it, 'An Englishman does not lie, but he would never dream of telling you the truth.' So much happens below the surface; as the English have cultivated the art, and the virtue, of surface politeness, it is often very distressing to find contempt, distrust, or dislike lurking beneath civility.

However, it is not only because of the English that objective criteria are difficult to establish; it is also because of the West Indians and the nature of the society from which they have come. In spite of the great emphasis the average West Indian (so far as he exists) places on open friendliness and a certain gay frankness that softens unpalatable truths or untruths, he can be as inward as any Englishman.

Dr. Philip Sherlock, in a broadcast, said:

The glory of being West Indians is that we have exploded the myth of racial superiority. The most significant thing about being West Indians is that our harmony of races does not come from tolerance, for there is nothing to be tolerated, nor from acceptance for there is nothing to be accepted; rather it springs out of natural human feeling, affection, respect, and this means all the more because it is we who have achieved this, we who know in our bodies and in the bodies of our fathers the meaning of discrimination, deprivations, agonies. . . .

Discrimination, deprivations, agonies, are a very real part of the West Indian situation, true though it is that we have much to teach the world. I found I sometimes presented two separate pictures of the West Indies in my conversations with friends: when we talked about the racial situation in the world the West Indies was an area of hope; when we talked about the West Indies in isolation it was a hot-bed of racial neuroses.

In *The Colour Problem*, Anthony Richmond has an excellent chapter on 'The Aftermath of Slavery in the West Indies' which contains these sentences:

While the colour conflict elsewhere takes the form of a struggle for power between the white man and the black, the conflict in the West Indies is the struggle going on within the personality of the Negro himself. Here more than anywhere, the legacy of slavery is to be observed. . . . Legal emancipation was not social or economic emancipation; still less was it psychological emancipation. . . . (p. 222)

Most West Indians I have met in Britain suffer from neuroses about colour. Partly they brought them to Britain, partly they found them there.

In talking about colour, as about anything important in human experience, complexity and ambiguity make a clear statement which is also honest and fairly complete very difficult indeed. I have often been uncertain about whether my hyper-sensitivity to situations involving colour—that is, to just about every situation I found myself in in Britain—had not distorted facts more than I knew.

I am hopeful, however. To set against most of my adverse judgements there was always an observation of what seemed more acceptable, there was a standard to judge by. If, for example, I say with any validity that some of my friends (subconsciously, perhaps even consciously) never managed to treat me as a person equal and basically similar, but always as a black man, theoretically equal but necessarily strange and alien, it is because I can say with certainty that some of my friends had more welcome attitudes.

On the subject of colour there was one white friend who was frequently helpful. Perhaps this was partly because he was from Kenya and was to some extent familiar with racial problems, though ones quite different from my own; perhaps partly because as a Jew he understood prejudice. His emotional honesty may, however, have had nothing to do with either of these facts.

Of my two other closest white friends, who were English, one was so free from colour that I rarely felt like imposing my neurotic worries on him; also, though he was often acute and often sympathetic, he made such a virtue of strength that my colour complexes may have seemed to him rather effete. The other, fine man as he was, never really forgot that I was black. He didn't mind that I was black, at least not consciously; but I think that he now and again felt good that he had gone deep enough to see beyond my blackness, blackness which always seemed very near the surface of his mind. Perhaps, too, it was too often near the surface of mine.

I was once making distinctions in this sort of way to my Kenyan friend when he found it necessary to tell me: 'But you *are* black!'

I had overdone the sensitivity; or his accusation was fair. He thought he detected some desire to be other than black, a wish to deny the physical fact. But what I had meant to talk about was not a physical fact but an emotional attitude to that fact. For himself, my Kenyan friend attached no more significance to the fact that I was black than to the fact that his girl-friend had brown hair or the fact that his father was bald.

This man sometimes understood me better than I liked. I remember one New Year's Eve finding myself at a loss for what to do in Oxford. I had been to see a film, and the girl I had taken was going to a small party to which I had not been invited. I decided to look up this friend of mine who lived not far from the theatre. It turned out there was to be a party in his building. I was reluctant to go and my friend knew why, perhaps more deeply than I myself knew at first. In a similar situation at home I would undoubtedly have gone to the party; the real reason for my reluctance was fear of rejection (nothing violent of course, just tacit disapproval) by a white host I had not met. I wanted my friend to check if it was all right to invite me to the party. In fact, I wanted him to ask because I was black and they were white; but I didn't expect him or want him to make an issue of my colour; in so far as my colour was an issue it must be kept discreet. If after the host had granted permission he was surprised or disappointed to find me black, so much the worse for him. But my friend, for all his intuitions, blundered this time. He told the host that I was black and more or less implied that he was asking him only to reassure himself that the host was not prejudiced.

Naturally the host was furious, as few people are prejudiced when you put any question like that.

There is a third, perhaps the greatest, difficulty in establishing criteria. Even when certain that some remark or act had distinguished me as *other*, I was often very unsure indeed whether this was because I was not English, because I was visibly not English, because I was not white, or because I was both not-English and not-white.

The English are notorious for xenophobia. I believe the notoriety to be well earned. Even when, as often, there is no deep-seated objection to a particular foreigner, there remains, I think, the tendency to dismiss all foreigners. Sometimes, indeed often, this was done in the form of a rather weak joke.

It is necessary to distinguish between jokes; but to understand what I mean you need to know something about the cycle of my integration into the small society of Oxford.

Sensibly, I think, when I arrived at Oxford I was determined not at first to spend much time with West Indians. For one thing, there were none living in my college except me. For another, I felt I already had a large number of West Indian friends and should take advantage of the chance to meet more non-West Indians. More important, however, was my awareness that the centre of Oxford life is the college and that I must become integrated in the college community; to go seeking out West Indian friends every time something troubled me would be foolish. So, though I was thankful for the friendship of more senior West Indians in Oxford, I did not at first seek them out. I accepted their invitations and invited them to tea or sherry (so quickly I learnt that very English reciprocity!) but I rarely called on them uninvited.

The process of integrating was slower than I had expected. I had come from the University College of the West Indies where students were nearly all West Indians. We made friends quickly in that society; this had its disadvantages, of course: mainly an almost complete lack of privacy. I learnt very soon how important to most Englishmen is the idea of privacy and the right to keep one's business to one's self. I learnt too how much more slowly friendship came in Oxford than at UCWI. At first I seemed to be progressing very rapidly; those I invited for coffee seemed to find me at least as interesting as I found them. Then I noticed that no one came uninvited; and I remembered that UCWI was very different. In my first term, except for those on specific business, only two men ever came to my room un-invited; and neither was English. I wondered whether I had been too friendly for the English: it was as though I had done some-thing like taking Hoffnung's ironic advice to visitors to Britain, 'On entering a railway carriage, make sure to shake hands with all the passengers.' Englishmen seemed not to understand that when I said 'Drop in any time', I meant it, that I did not mean the sort of vague invitation well-mannered Englishmen offer only during awkward pauses.

In this matter, as in so many others, there was an irony. Things improved in the second term and by the third term I knew who my friends were. I mentioned my first-term worry to one of them. He pointed out to me that he had issued several open invitations I had not taken up; my reticence had been of the same quality as theirs. Not entirely, I think. Their worry was fear of intruding; mine, fear of rejection.

I was not, however, rejected. The mass of men in my college treated me as another individual, didn't really care where I came from but knew instead that I read English, spoke badly at the Debating Society, was often listening at the Union, played keen hockey and was an asset to the college at tennis. By the middle of the third term of my first year I felt well integrated. There was no difficulty about loyalties because the loyalties were too small to conflict with my fundamental loyalty to the West Indies; I could be loyal to my college, as I was, without being any less loyal to my country. I could even, if I wished (and, except during Varsity matches, I did not wish), be loyal to my university; though as I had come from UCWI, that was more complicated.

So, integrated into Oxford society I was. I found I had a few firm friends and the certainty of them made it easy to have many more casual friends who made no demands on me and on whom I made no demands.

The integration had not been achieved at the expense of my West Indianness. However, my West Indianness had, I felt, been somewhat in abeyance in my first year; I was West Indian but probably it was to many people more important that I read English and I lived in St. Edmund Hall.

I believe the process of my development was a process towards a more assertive West Indianness. Paradoxically, the more integrated I became, the more aware I was of not belonging. Possibly because the more integrated I became the more people expected me to share not just their small loyalties but their bigger loyalties and their unpalatable assumptions. Also, once the basic point had been made that as a West Indian I was very familiar with English and British culture, had in fact been nursed on it, it became more and more necessary to establish that in spite of this I was different. Partly, the pressure came from within. One detected an assumption one did not share which one was thought to share. Also, probably my closest friends were Conservative in their politics and my instincts were very anti-Conservative; the Conservatives always seemed to me—I still think they are—very like the worst of a complacent, bloated West Indian middle-class, though, I confess, more intelligent. However, their intelligence seemed often directed to justifying theories of class superiority which my own nature and my best friends at UCWI had taught me to despise. There was a need, then, to speak out and assert my differentness. And if I was to assert my differentness, why not my identity? And what was my identity?

I am a West Indian, more fervent than the facts of our culture may support. But I believe that the difference between us and the British from whom much of our present culture derives, or the Africans or the Indians or the Chinese or the Portuguese or the French, is enough to justify an awareness of separate identity. Somehow, in spite of my internal dialogue about colour conflicts and colonial complexes, it does not embarrass me to like many facets of English culture. I can enjoy poets as English as William Cowper and John Betjeman. It does not embarrass me to read and to use English. (One of Lamming's finest observations, is, for me, that English is a West Indian language.)

The West Indies has a complex about things English, as though England were the only place from which we have borrowed. It does not worry anybody that our Anancy stories in Jamaica are from Africa, because the mass of us are of African origin and some of us wish to remember only our African roots, to exclude all the other forces that have moulded our present.

To return to jokes. There are jokes that include and jokes that exclude; it may be the same joke that does either, at different times.

Soon after I arrived in England, to make a joke about my difference—my non-Englishness or my colour—was to include me, because it made me the focus of a social activity, laughter among friends; provided, of course, that the intention was not plainly derisive. To make that same joke two years later was to exclude me, because I and others had come to take my belonging for granted and to focus on my difference was to point out that in many ways I did not really belong. One friend in particular was often guilty of excluding me in this way. Although he accepted me as a friend, he always regarded me as *other*, and, pretending to be so completely liberated that he could poise himself on the precipice of bad taste, he often made jokes about my colour. He was right, of course, that to make easy jokes about colour is to show that one is not a slave to it. But the jokes must be easy and it is best that they be funny. To make a poor joke now and again is quite normal, but to make even good jokes constantly about any one subject, is to suggest not liberation but subconscious enslavement seeking to prove itself freedom on a conscious level.

The trouble, too, with most of the jokes was that they did not focus on me as West Indian, which I was always proud to avow, but on me as black; and I was not normally particularly proud of being black, though not, I hope, ashamed either.

Sometimes, too, the jokes assumed that I was African. I am not African and my reaction to many Africans worries me. The

Africans I like are, frankly, the ones I would have mistaken for West Indian students; they are coloured and have an ease with English manners which seems inherited. I think I could like, too, the militant African, preoccupied with injustice, fiercely preaching the equality of all men. But I met in England one or two Africans who embarrassed me; they tried to accept Englishness but failed badly. I once had the excruciating experience of listening to an African say thanks to a Rotary Club in Wales for an evening's entertainment (in fact, for two cups of coffee, sandwiches and cakes) and pledge his undying gratitude to them for their great kindness. Although I am well aware, on an intellectual level, that there is no such simple thing, culturally, as 'an African', that you need (at the very least) to place him on the continent; and that, further, when you had placed him, this African would only be *an* African, not proto-anything, I am trying to be honest about my emotional revulsion to many of the Africans I met. Of the two I liked most, one had a West Indian girl-friend and could easily be thought West Indian himself, the other had an Oxford blue and a charming reserve which marked him out as different from many others I had met.

Lamming makes a good comment on this matter. He quotes Naipaul only to destroy him. Naipaul wrote: 'It is not fully realized how completely the West Indian Negro identifies himself with England . . . Africa has been forgotten; films about African tribesmen excite derisive West Indian laughter.' Lamming comments justly: 'It is precisely because Africa has not been forgotten that the West Indian embarrassment takes the form of derisive laughter.'

I think there was something similar in my reaction to Africans. Those I did not like seemed to be letting the side down if they were not smooth enough for my English-biased taste. For whenever there was another Black around I was, and knew I was, a Black. Very few Englishmen distinguished between us. The need was, therefore, for some proving of myself, some acuteness, some witticism, some easy friendliness, some international sophistication.

West Indians have, I think, a certain genealogical justification for preaching international anything.

I am very dark brown, not black as midnight (or five-past, like that Selvon character). When I have been playing tennis in the sun I get darker and very shiny. Someone who knew little about the West Indies might reasonably assume that my ancestors were African slaves. So they were, I think, but on one side only. My grandmother's (my mother's mother's) complexion was as near European pinko-grey as doesn't matter and her features were scarcely negroid; she claimed we have Irish ancestors. I hope I don't seem to want to lighten my colour by appealing to my grandparents. This is somehow the sort of thing that nobody does in the West Indies. What they still do, though less often than they did, is marry fair-skinned Negroes to 'lighten the colour' of their children; and also many people delight to show that Mrs. X is not really white at all, in spite of what seems to be, as her grandfather was Negro.

Now and again in England I was positively proud of being black. When I saw *Raisin In The Sun*, the play, which the critics had panned, I was proud of being able to understand what they had failed to understand. The central accuracy of that play is that its conflicts are mainly internal ('the struggle going on within the personality of the Negro himself'). It was moving to see his search for identity (which always seems to lead to a flirtation with an African past), his search for integrity (which he can find only in his treatment of a particular situation, and not as Negro but as man). I was proud, too, when I saw the Senegal dancers at the New Theatre in Oxford. So much of the programme seemed to relate to what I had seen in the West Indies, and I saw then the distinctive beauty of black bodies—which somehow had not previously struck me, and I think I had some insight into that occasional oneness among Negroes which has been erected into the concept of *négritude*. It is at moments such as several during that performance that one feels an especial fondness for the African elements of the West Indian past which survive in the West Indian present. The programme reminded me that rhythmical black bodies are a thing of which I am part.

Here and there a play reminded me that I was a West Indian, not just a black. I had read Errol John's *Moon On A Rainbow Shawl* and was consequently appalled, when I saw it on the stage, that it had been given to non-Trinidadian principals, one of whom was American; for the great virtue of John's play is its fidelity to Trinidadian speech. I missed the television production, which friends told me was much better, with Errol John himself taking one of the leads. Barry Reckord's play, *You In Your Small Corner*, I enjoyed very much too. It really has little to do with miscegenation and much more to do with class prejudice; only our colour conditioning makes it seem odd that middle-class Blacks should look down on working-class Whites. One of the reviews, an obtuse and wilful one by W. A. Darlington in the *Daily Telegraph*, reminded me that I was black as well as West Indian. The critic had an aversion to miscegenation which he made no attempt to channel through relevant comment on the play. Alan Brien, writing in the *Spectator* on another play touching on miscegenation, *Hot Summer Night* by Ted Willis, had the intelligence to see that the answer to 'My daughter wants to marry a West Indian' must always be 'Which West Indian?'

In inter-racial matters, as in all human relations, nothing should replace the personal. Too often, one accepts a generalization that does not accord with personal experience. Where this is a well-documented statement by an expert this is all right; but too often it is something less respectable.

I found I learnt only very slowly to be cautious about generalizing. I was always meeting exceptions. If I agreed that public-school men are reserved I was likely to become friendly with one who soon told me his life story. If I said that Northerners are frank I was likely to discover from closer friendship that the Northerners I knew were as careful as anybody else what they said to whom. It is bad enough when one generalizes and is wrong; when one makes uncharitable generalizations denied by one's experience, this is far worse.

It is not easy to avoid this. I was always falling into it, confusing the Imperialist Colonialist Rulers with the man in the street. For a long time I found that although I had many English friends whenever I spoke about 'the English' my comment was unfriendly. A Jamaican friend of mine said to me: 'I am an anglophile, but I don't like English men.' Her attitude was far clearer than mine, as it could be taken to be a distinction between English ways and English people; mine was a tendency to generalize from other people's observations. But I can be defended. For another difficulty in establishing the objective criteria I keep explaining that I cannot establish, is that the people I met or the people I got to know were necessarily those with less prejudice rather than more prejudice. Life could seem fairly rosy if I concentrated only on Oxford and the people I stayed with outside it.

I know, however, from reading and from talking to other West Indians, that London can be very difficult. In Oxford when I needed accommodation I was lucky enough to know a West Indian moving out of suitable digs, and so I took them when he had left. Our landlady was pleasant and unprejudiced, and the rent was reasonable. But I have friends who have scoured London for flats and found time after time that landladies who on the telephone seemed eager enough for a new tenant found that the flat had been taken in the twenty minutes it had taken to get to it from the phone.

The concrete, and, so to speak, certifiable instances of prejudice I have encountered are three only; though, as I have indicated, there were many others which are arguable.

The first occurred during my first Michaelmas vacation, when I was in London. This was the year of Notting Hill and so possibly there was still a good deal of tension. I was on my way by tube to the West End and I had to wait on a platform to change trains. There were some Teddy Boys near by; they seemed very noisy, singing and laughing. I looked at them. I have no idea whether my glance was contemptuous; it was not meant to be. It seemed that one of the group, a flimsy lad (I thought), disliked me looking at them. When we got on the crowded train he stared at me and I stared back at him. This seemed to have been too much for him. He attempted to move in my direction, muttering, I thought, 'Black bastard!' As the train was crowded there was no question of him getting at me. However, a larger, apparently better-adjusted lad, restrained him, commenting, 'He's the same colour as Louis Armstrong, man.' The simple reasoning appeared to satisfy the aggressive one. I thought it significant that the peacemaker should have chosen to make peace in this way, through the inter-racial symbol of a jazz hero.

The second incident connects with Oxford, but not intimately. I was at the Folkestone Hockey Festival with the St. Edmund Hall team. Most of us decided to go to a jazz club, and we duly became members (to ensure admittance). I danced with one or two girls there, not entirely without tenseness, and then I approached a girl who had her back half-turned to me. More or less over her shoulder I said, 'May I?' She turned with her arms in the ready position for dancing and then saw I was black. Her confusion was lamentable. She muttered something that must have been an apology, and fled.

In the relations between West Indians and women in Britain I think I have seen vestiges of colonialism. It was very common during and just after the war for servicemen to bring home to Jamaica white English wives. Some of these marriages were true marriages based on love and friendship and they have survived in our multi-racial society. However, some of these marriages were attempts by white-biased Negroes to raise their status in a shade-conscious society. Many of these have ended in disaster. I do not think the tendency to marry Whites for the wrong reasons is as strong as it was, but it seems to me to have been replaced in some university towns by sexual colour-discrimination. Comparatively speaking, the argument seems to run, West Indian women may be treated with respect, but the English, Scottish and Irish women who date coloured West Indians want only to test the mythical Negro virility and should be given at the earliest opportunity the chance to do so. The slave seduces the master. A West Indian can hardly be blamed for despising a woman who deep down regards him not as a man but as a foreign phallus.

Some West Indian–English sexual relationships, let me hasten to add, have, of course, none or little of this debasing quality; I do not wish to be thought to say more than I have said. I do not dislike mixed marriages, nor would I advise against them. The big difficulty in black–white man–woman relationships in Britain seems to be that British women know that because of common prejudice there are social dangers in dating a black man, and so only the emotionally involved, the mentally liberated or the sexually abandoned think it worth the risk. I doubt that very many of the mentally liberated failed to fall into either of the other categories. It seemed rare to find a close inter-sex relationship which was simply a friendship, not a love-affair or a bed-arrangement.

The third certifiable incident of prejudice had to do with tennis. I had played lawn-tennis for Oxford in 1959 and was playing again in 1960. Every two years Oxford and Cambridge combined play Harvard and Yale, alternately in the United States and in Britain. I was competing for a place on the team to America, and so was an Indian from Cambridge whose position was even more certain. Imagine our surprise, then, when, in mid-season, our captains told us that the Lawn Tennis Association had decided that only Englishmen should be considered for the combined team, as the tour was in the interest of English tennis and Anglo-American relations. It was embarrassing for the captains who were both, I think, above colour discrimination. I was not entirely fair to the Oxford captain: I did not tell him that my keenness to compete for the trip had been largely due to the encouragement of a West Indian tennis player who had captained Cambridge only a few years earlier and had gone to America on the tour. He had been, however, white. White, too, had been the Jamaican who had gone on the tour before. I accepted the decision easily, as it is always easy to accept facts which your friends deplore and treatment which they acknowledge as unjust. As it happened, the captains must have argued the matter further, for the L.T.A. reversed their decision. In the end, the Indian went and I did not. I was disappointed, but had no reason to believe that I had been unfairly treated; our three members were our two best players and our captain who led the combined side. What is most interesting about this incident is the early obtuseness of the L.T.A. officials in imagining that anybody intelligent enough to get into Oxford or Cambridge could swallow so ridiculous a reason, or the callousness with which they dared to send us a reason they knew we would recognize as dishonest. Such, no doubt, are the ways of English officialdom. No doubt they said they were not prejudiced themselves but that their neighbours the Americans might not like to entertain coloured players. There is a brilliant little quotation in Ruth Glass's *The Newcomers* from a novel by A. G. Bennett:

Since I come 'ere I never met a single English person who 'ad any colour prejudice. Once, I walked the whole length of a street looking for a room, and everyone told me that he or she 'ad no prejudice against coloured people. It was the neighbour who was stupid. . . . Neighbours are the worst people to live beside in this country.

From reading and from conversation one of the things that strikes me most about the English is their moral blindness to certain issues. The *New Statesman* and the *Observer* and *The Times* may tell them firmly what is happening; many people sophisticated enough to read these papers will never believe them. Some Englishmen even defend this self-deception. Much as I enjoy reading F. L. Lucas, who writes so wittily and so well, the following paragraph from his essay on Johnson is an embarrassment:

The English are perhaps specially prone to self deception. We have a reputation for mental dishonesty. And it is an unpleasant one. Still this vice may be, in part, due to a virtue. It could be argued that there is more public and private conscience in England than in some countries; and this develops greater skill in lulling conscience asleep, subtler forms of cant. And again this vice may have in it a certain utility—the English often behave as shabbily as any other civilized nation; but, because they so successfully convince themselves that they are behaving well, they do, in fact, become less demoralized, less cynical, from behaving badly.

This blindness or dishonesty can produce classics such as the statement by somebody or other when it was proposed to move a family of Indians on to a housing estate in 1961: 'This is not a matter of colour prejudice, we just don't want coloured families living on our estate.' The speaker is very clear where moral right lies; but he fails to connect the principle with the particular situation.

The same sort of process appeared in the Tory Government's Immigrants Bill for which they denied any basis of colour-discrimination. I have said it is often difficult to separate the Englishman's reaction to a foreigner from his reaction to a Black, but a Bill of this sort makes it much easier.

Is it paradoxical that with the widespread self-deception (the advantages of which have been so charmingly argued by Mr. Lucas) there should go a preoccupation with being moral leaders of the world? Without pausing to tidy their own house—to make colour discrimination in public establishments illegal, for example—British leaders hurry about to point out, with fine politeness and infinite tact, that other houses are not clean. That they are often right only seems to highlight their extraordinary blindness at home.

In one of his essays, Robert Lynd has amusingly explored the English tendency to assume that all the virtues of mankind are distinctively English and consequently to dub all vices 'un-English'. Lynd tells the story of a Dutch captain before a (North-ern Irish) magistrate; one of his men had been involved in a brawl in which he was alleged to have bitten a man. The magis-trate said: 'It is very un-English to bite people, and I would like you to impress it on your men.' To which the Dutch captain replied, equally gravely: 'It is very un-Dutch, too, your worship.' Calling vices un-English is one indication of that willingness to exclude foreigners from an English universe, for, in expressing universal values in parochial terms, it extends the possibility of agreement only to the English and those who love them.

There were several organizations which seemed devoted to *including* foreigners and to increasing the number who love England. It was through the finest of the ones I had anything to do with, the Dominions Fellowship Trust, now unfortunately defunct, that I came to meet some of the families whose friendship I still value. The excellence of the D.F.T. was its personal nature. The ladies who ran it made a point of meeting singly or in small parties the students or visitors to Britain whom they hoped to help; in fact, I am not sure that they helped people they had not managed to meet. They tried to find out what sort of person you were and what were your interests, so that they could get you invited to a home you would fit into. Their accuracy was uncanny. While it may be valuable, as other organizations—and, indeed, the D.F.T. from time to time—did, to herd people together for large teas or cocktail parties or to run them around the country in busloads, these arrangements often seem more like charity than friendship because they are necessarily impersonal; one does not like to be one unit deployed with a lot of other units. Large teas and large cocktail parties are not the ideal circumstances for meeting foreign students: some of them are uncomfortable in those surroundings and may be a little suspicious of charitable advances; others who seem to relax have probably learnt not to take people seriously at cocktail parties. Also, many of the people at these parties work too hard at being friendly to the foreigners; this sets up reactions which make real contact impossible.

The British Council was usually better than the amateur organizations. Though some of its personnel were not exactly lovable, most of them managed to be helpful without being archly friendly; an approach much better for a foreigner's self-respect. The British Council gave us the chance to do many of the things we wanted to do and to visit many of the places we wanted to visit. Taking up one of those offers, and having to pay modestly for some wonderful opportunity—perhaps a course at Stratford which gave you good seats to all the season's productions; or well chosen tickets for the Edinburgh Festival—you felt no discomfort, because you were not often aware of patronage.

I know that some organizations have seen that it is inadvisable to have hostels for foreign students only, as these hostels are isolated from the British community. I know, from staying in one of them, that the effect on the students can be very serious indeed, especially, I suppose, in a large city like London. At a British Council hostel I stayed at, there seemed to be many foreigners, mostly Blacks, who had never really met an Englishman, and certainly had no English friends (except, here and there, a sleeping partner). They talked about the coldness of the English, about the hypocrisy of the English, almost entirely from encounters with prospective landladies, with the hostel staff and with their classmates who never invited them home.

I am not at all happy about what I have heard of the quota-system, twenty per cent. English persons in every hostel. When the relationship is worked out obviously in this way, two main effects seem very possible: that the sort of Englishman who enters this type of hostel may have a false idea of his function, may believe that he is representing England and must practise hands-across-the-seamanship, when, in fact, he would do most good by ignoring, just as he would ignore Englishmen, those foreigners he did not like and making friends with those he did; and that the foreigners may distrust the English placed with them and feel that they are there as educators and uplifters rather than as fellow-students in need of accommodation. To put it simply, the arrangement may well seem unnatural, and only unselfconsciousness can make it helpful. I confess, though, that even a strict twenty per cent. sort of arrangement is much better than an all-foreign hostel run by fatherly or disagreeable officials. It is good for foreigners at least to meet some Englishmen so that they may have a particular basis for their views instead of exchanging crude prejudices.

I have been luckier than many Englishmen in the range of my social contacts. As a foreigner I could move through all classes (where particular persons would have me) for I belonged to none. I have friends who would, I think, be uncomfortable in each others' homes. People were at a loss to know where to place me in the class-gradation.

Friends invited me to spend time in their homes. I have been happy in most and uncomfortable in none. Families were often less selfconscious than the friends themselves. Friends were sometimes uneasy about whether I and their families would get on together; but this worry usually had nothing to do with my being either foreign or black, facts no doubt well appreciated when the invitation was made.

I think I have noticed everywhere a tendency towards contempt of other classes and groups and a quickness with dismissive judgements.

There was a man in our college from Latin America; he had the sort of swarthy skin that would tan easily, his hair was thick and long and seemed greasy; he often wore tight jeans and a sweater. One day he was crossing the quad. I remarked to a public-school friend of mine that this man was Latin American. 'Oh,' he said, 'I shall have to revise my opinion of him completely.' He had never actually spoken to the man. Strangely, his attitude was not entirely unreasonable; for if the Latin American had been an Englishman then his dressing as he did would almost certainly have meant he was not the sort of person with whom my Conservative friend would normally wish to associate.

No matter what you dislike, it is clear that three years in England cannot leave you unaffected. I think I have changed in some ways. Not in simple ways such as tending to let my hair grow longer before I cut it (as was necessary, since English barbers still don't know how to cut Negro hair and my West Indian barber lived in London). I have, I suspect, become a little more reserved; I dislike more the constant prying of a small society, the sort of claustrophobia the small society can impose; I have developed my sense of irony more and am more capable of civilized nastiness than I was; I think I understand my identity a bit better.

Perhaps I understand, too, the subtlety of being West Indian. And I learnt the fundamental lesson of nationalism. I learnt this half an hour away from England, approaching the cliffs of Dover. There was excitement among the English on board. I looked, but the cliffs seemed very ordinary to me. And then I realized that of course the cliffs are not cliffs: to the Englishmen they are a

C

symbol of something greater, of the return from a land of strangers, of the return home. Nothing is more important in nationalism than the feeling of ownership. The definitions may be of intellectual interest but they cannot hold a nation together. The important thing about the West Indies, or Jamaica, is that it is ours. We need now to persuade all our people that this is really so.

2

The Colour Problem at the University: A West Indian's Changing Attitudes

KENNETH RAMCHAND

Trinidad

Kenneth Ramchand was born in Trinidad in 1939. He completed his early education there. Between 1959 and 1963 he was at the University of Edinburgh where he took his M.A. Honours in English and gained a Mackenzie Scholarship in English from the university. He is at present engaged in post-graduate work on the West Indian novel. He hopes to lecture and teach in the West Indies.

THE paperback edition of the West Indian sees him as indulging in exotic calypso colours of red and green and yellow, riotous colours that compel attention, loud colours that are taken to indicate a coarseness of visual palate, or an eye unaware of pattern and design, and unable to discriminate between variant shades of the same colour. ('You West Indians,' in despair, 'you cannot appreciate Art, you only look for the bright colours.')

If this popular image is valid, we find in the West Indian an amazing double-vision. For, in the contemplation of human groups, no society has evolved a more delicate instrument of perception. The West Indian consciousness suspends, in equipoise, considerations of racial origin and considerations of degrees of blackness. In looking at the complex construct that is colonial society, it blends elements from these categories with rare flexibility.

The initial breakdown is along lines of known racial origin. Here are some children at play:

> 'Nigger is a nation, They stink with perspiration' (African)
> 'Coolie, coolie, Come for roti' (Indian)
> 'Chinee chinee never die, Flat nose and Chinky eye' (Chinese)
> 'Whitey cock-o-roach' (Not very sure)

This crude analysis is refined by a delicate perception of the variants of skin colour. At one end of the scale is 'White'(roughly = English). Next come 'West Indian Whites' (diverse European origin, many now carrying in their blood the secret of their fathers' dark connexions). After these come the 'light-skinned' or 'yellow' Chinese. Then come the black ones—Indians and Africans. Of the infinite mixtures available, all that can be said is that there is an intuitive apprehension, and a certain placing of every possible variant along the colour scale. 'Black' is complex indeed. An Indian may be black, but his highest degree of blackness is indicated in the taunt, 'Look at you, you just like a nigger.' In West Indian society, 'black' is usually reserved for 'Negro', and 'Negro' ranges from the 'tar baby' of the West Indian Reader, to the 'red nigger'. It is even possible to be blacker than black: in a book by the Trinidadian Samuel Selvon, one character is called 'Midnight' because he is the blackest in his group. A new figure comes along however, and he, impossibly, is blacker still. The delicate instrument reacts sensitively; the new man is christened 'Five-past-twelve'.

Leaving the West Indies and coming to Britain is like entering a land where the natives suffer from a curious kind of colour blindness in the contemplation of human groups. This special form of blindness manifests itself in an insensitivity to racial discriminations and variant shades within the category 'black'. It registers two crude categories, black and white.

The West Indian consciousness is outraged by the crudity of the categorization. In the rarefied atmosphere of the mother country, the delicate instrument ceases to function. All West Indians are black. Under impartial pressure, the first defensive measure is the formation of West Indian groups and a kind of recognition, at last, of West Indian community.

There is another useful by-product of the coming face-to-face with the colour problem. The denial of variant shades within the category 'black' in metropolitan society sharpens the vision of the West Indian. The West Indian comes to realize that if society in Britain tended to glance at the physical characteristics of groups instead of focusing upon the behaviour of the individual, the same was true of society in the West Indies. In the colonial society, the way of looking at groups was not more delicate than the distortion of the personal realities in Britain. It was only less crude. For instead of living with individuals both societies were reckoning with stereotypes.

This sketching in of the background has invited observation of the delicacy of colour perception in West Indian society, and the crudeness of colour categorization in British society, but it has indicated that the same basic fallacy—attention to the physical characteristics of groups—has marred the vision of both societies. It thus provides adequate justification for the largely personal nature of most of what follows. It is only through a series of descriptions of personal experience that the colour problem can be seen in operation. Moreover, it is felt that to set down an individual response and reflections arising out of personal involvement with people and situations in an uncensored form, would not only give the kind of insight into aspects of the colour problem which becomes crude in the analysis, but it would catch the subtle movements by which shifts of attitudes may take place. The recording consciousness may itself be a product of the apprehension of a colour problem.

As I stood on the deck of the S.S. *Antilles*, Trinidad grew smaller and smaller, and I of the big dreams reminded myself of my obligations:

'Boy, you goin' England, ah want you to eat book, don't let nobody beat you in exams nuh.'

'Woman like bush up dey, partner. They like the black boys too bad.'

'You better watch out, you hear, dey beatin' black fellers with all kind a bicycle chain up there dese days.'

'Don't let them make you feel small man; if you look good you go see this whiteness is really a kind of skin disease all of them have.'

I knew well what I wanted of 'England', but long before I got to Southampton I was overwhelmed by the certainty of my inability to cope with the books, the bicycle chains and the sex-starved natives.

At Southampton, I determined to survive. The customs officer stood before me and stuck his little list in my face. I read, and turned my eyes away. Four years later, he spoke, 'Have you read the list?' . . . Yes bwana, yes. . . .

Waterloo, London. A Jamaican porter approached. I ignored him and selected an English one. . . . My coolie. A big tip for you today. . . . All around, white faces closing in, and, at the last moment, going past. And then the man with the ready-made smile. The British Council man.

The West Indian's ambivalent attitude to the British Council provides a major insight into the colour problem. The British Council exists to provide organized kindness at five shillings a year. As such, it satisfies felt needs. Because the organization supplies needs which in an integrated society would have found fulfilment in human relationships, it remains, like the accommodating woman, curiously unloved, even in use.

Soon, I was on the train to Waverley, Edinburgh. In my single compartment I began to think of home, but half-way to the Scottish capital, a middle-aged man with dirty nostrils and no hair silently joined me. He seemed annoyed with himself for having intruded on my privacy, and so, all the way to Waverley he sat there looking sick (he in his corner, I in mine) in penitential silence.

Waverley at last. The man with the ready-made smile again, and in minutes I was listening to my very first landlady. I was going to be happy with her. She always preferred my kind. We were so polite. . . . 'Mornin' ma'am. . . .'

I set all these things down as they strike me in retrospect, or as I might have re-lived them, after four years. At the time they were allowed to pass. My real concern at first was to avoid the bicycle chains and to watch out for the sex-starved females. As neither threatened on this first day, I wrote to Trinidad to say that I had arrived safely. I paused to look at my skin for signs of the disease, but I was as black as ever. I decided not to make that report yet. One never knew: perhaps next morning I would awake to find myself infected.

The weeks passed and the fear of the bicycle chain diminished. Violence, it seemed, occurred only in Nottingham where the workers were fighting for women and wages. In the liberal atmosphere of an ancient university one can always avoid violence by not walking too late at night.* I soon reminded myself that for four years I was to live in this land: I must not only avoid hostilities, I must invite friendships.

And so, I groomed myself (one lock of hair carefully out of place) and attended the Freshers' dance. In the huge hall, there was country dancing and shrieks of delight. Carnival, I thought. Suddenly, I felt like jumping too. I approached an approach-worthy young lady with my best smile (the lips pulled a little to the right). She was so tired. A few seconds later, she was throwing those shapely legs about in what was, presumably, a Highland fling. Her dancing partner had a fat face and straggly hair. My face was lean and youthful. My hair jet black. And my teeth were the colour of pearl. . . . But who can fathom the mind of a beautiful woman?

My next move was to join the West Indian Association.

For a year I stuck firmly to the group. For a year I had lunch with West Indians, coffee with West Indians, dates with West Indians and I attended purely West Indian parties. At the lectures I had one friend—a brave little girl whom I got to know and like well over the years. But, as in those early days I never dared disturb the universe, our relationship remained firmly platonic. Among the men, a war veteran, with memories of pre-war cricket, was my only ally.

Outside the university, matters were about to take a strange turn. I had already spent three months in the country, and having

* Last summer, a Jamaican student returning home late at night from a visit to some domino-playing friends was assaulted by a gang of youths.

concluded that the bicycle chain did not, as it were, apply to the university student, I was about to put a similar colophon to the subject of sex-starved females. But one night, a friend arrived in a hurry.

'Want to come and meet a little thing?'

'Well . . . nothing to do.'

'Come on.'

He went to the telephone booth, this midnight, talked for a while, and then beckoned me.

'Come,' he said, 'she want to talk to you.'

'But . . . she don't know me. . . .'

'What the . . .'

I picked up the phone, searched for my best accent, and my sexiest tone, and waited:

'So you're coming along.'

'Ye-es.' (Coolly.)

'Why?'

'You never know!' (Wittily.)

'You want Scotch and Scottish hospitality?'

'Yes,' (my God) I sighed, 'yes.'

We were on our way.

'Look nuh man, I don't want no prostitute, you know.'

'Easy, clot. You young. These ain't no prostitutes.'

Who were they?

For a variety of reasons, women at the university are reluctant to form relationships with coloured students. It seemed natural at first, to expect that since one spent so much time at the university, one's friends both male and female would come from the university, for it is here, we are told, that personal contacts are made, here that minds meet. It became apparent, however, that there existed a tribe of nurses, *au pair* girls, typists, shop-assistants, one or two divorcées, a few erring wives, a nympho-maniac and various rejected university girls who satisfied the emotional needs of coloured students. Many of these girls are decent girls, and the degree of promiscuity varies. Many are intelligent people. Some are victims of their own loneliness, and some are victims of the coloured men's loneliness. Many are unloved. Some are loved for a time. A few become happy wives. The overall impression, however, is that a hasty sexual connexion has taken the place of any settled human relationship between black men and white women.

The deep malaise in the man–woman relationship involving coloured men and white women is paralleled by a total absence of relationships between white men and coloured women. This is a phenomenon that needs investigation by itself. In the days of the plantation, white men satisfied organic needs on slave women. No doubt, the prevailing attitude that white men only associate with black women for possible exotic sexual thrills, is a kind of deterrent to many white students. Probably too, if there were more black women at the university, the chances of a white man–black woman relationship would be increased, at least statistically.

The relationship between white men and black men at the university seems to be, strangely, a kind of passing acquaintance. In four undergraduate years, I count three lasting male friendships, but a series of inquiries among West Indians at the university reveals my personal experience to be unusual. Here is a typical example:

'Have you any good British friends?'

'No.'

'How come, man?'

'I never put myself out of the way to make friends. If nobody want to make friends with me, I don't want to make friends with them.'

The attitude is powerfully defensive. Behind it is a mind which has been antagonized, or at least, thinks it has been antagonized, by the suspicion of an unspoken attitude. Friendship, in the words of C. S. Lewis, is, 'in a sense not at all derogatory to it, the least natural of loves; the least instinctive, organic, biological, gregarious and necessary'. Eros, the love relationship, on the other hand, is, partly a matter for the nervous system. A woman may, therefore, as many women do, have a conflict between a state of mind and a state of feeling in relation to a black man. In a fair number of cases, feeling triumphs over mental attitude. But in a relationship between man and man (homosexuality apart) it is attitude which tells. Lack of a common interest upon which friendship may be built indicates, at the university, an unhappy kind of coexistence merely. The personal contact is possible, but this is only geographical. Common interests and friendships are not allowed to develop. This refusal to make friends is to be seen as part of a mental attitude to the black man, in the case of the man–man relationship, unhampered, as it were, by emotion. It is, in other words, a studied restraint.

The attitude of the British male undergraduates, within the field of reference of this essay, carries a strong load of sexual fear and jealousy: it expresses itself in a strict slating of female offenders against an unspoken masculine code. The university woman who forms a possible love relationship with a coloured man is quietly ostracized. The male of the species considers her contaminated by a phallic performer, the West Indian. And so, sexual rivalry takes the form of contemptuous non-competition and boycott. One of the main factors behind the reluctance of the female is the intransigence of the male. The white man–black man relationship is rare, and the black man–white woman relationship is heavily censored. Thus it comes about that the macabre sexual relationship outside the university (already described) has to carry those strains that might have been borne easily within the campus, as well as the strains set up by a lack of man–man contact. The sexual connexion quickly becomes a desperate struggle in the dark to hold on to sanity. It becomes a cure for all ills. It becomes a furious masturbation.

The gradual revelation of the weakness of human relationships between white and black students at the university, and the realization that this state of affairs has created a grotesque parody of the man–woman relationship, are the major discoveries of the West Indian student. It must be emphasized that the breakdown is not complete, and that there are mature men and women in all the faculties. But it is the discoveries which are highly influencing, and they are mainly responsible for a radical shift of attitude to the colour problem. One's original conception of the colour problem was that it operated where there was little opportunity for personal contact and where the educational level was low. But after coming to Britain, one discovers that the conception was naïve, the reality was confusing. For to experience four years at the university is to progress in a kind of forbidden knowledge from dreams of rich and edifying personal contact, towards disillusionment and cynicism. Education and personal contact are not allowed to become a moving force: the follow-through is checked, defensively. One may be safe from violence, but one is exposed to a more subtle variation of the colour bar.

This new knowledge has brought a touchiness to the eater of the forbidden fruit, which, with increasing insight into the motives of his white fellow student, translates itself into a desperate kind of self-scrutiny. He, thus, becomes more and more conscious that the association of black with inferiority dies hard. As the self-scrutiny becomes more intense, he begins to be aware of a wastage of the opportunities for personal contact, by a sabotage of the West Indian personality, and its distribution into functions. The West Indian is becoming more and more aware of himself as being cast in the role of performer. The audience is physically close but the social distance is great.

The new technique of looking at the black man operates at all levels.

On the academic level a successful West Indian becomes a phenomenon to those who notice: 'How *can* you be so *clever*?' The performance has a touch of the exotic in it, and somehow this has caused a lowering of the standards. Intelligence, by a mental flick of the wrist, becomes cleverness, a gimmick, and success has nothing to do with effort. (Sometimes the effort is granted, but it is turned around and seen as aggressiveness. Honest effort is impossible for the man who has to prove he is a man!) The successful West Indian is either clever (a man with a gimmick) or a performer in his own special field (a non-competitor) or at least, 'an uncharacteristic West Indian', that non-defining definition.

At Edinburgh, the West Indian calypso band is the most popular student band: all, performers. Other West Indians either play cricket or sing calypsoes. Those who cannot sing are disc-jockeys. It is regrettable that these appointed roles are accepted so readily. But the temptation is great.

The West Indian, as performer, is an image borrowed from the cricket field. Shackleton is an intelligent bowler, and Wesley Hall is a magnificent specimen (potent West Indian). Close is a player of character and determination, Sobers is a *natural* stroker of the ball. Meanwhile, we hear from afar that Peter Pollick is the fastest white bowler in the world, black bowlers being non-competitors.

At a party last year, I was introduced to an obscure gentleman:

'Do you play in the band?'

'No.' (With resentment.)

'Do you play cricket, then?'

'No.' (Amused.)

Long silence.

'Cheerio.'

He had scrutinized my personality and found it wanting.

One is either a performer or one has no personality. So far has the fragmentation proceeded.

There are no more bicycle chains. For the performers, there is applause, and after the show, social distance. The fear of physical violence is largely replaced in the individual consciousness by the fear of this new attempt to see the West Indian as performer, for this implies a kind of fragmentation, in the mind of the viewer, of the West Indian personality, a fragmentation which is a steady refusal to see the black man as a whole individual. It is, in fact, the old concept of black inferiority in a new, sophisticated form, appropriate to a centre of higher learning.

The symptoms of racial prejudice at the university are hard to discern. One finds oneself looking not for scars on one's own body, but for an attitude determining the behaviour of one's fellow students. At best, there is, after the suspicion, an un-provable certainty that there are large numbers of people at the university who constitutionally assume white superiority and its corollary. Over against this, and acting as a kind of foil to it, is another certainty—the presence of a small number who do see the black man as a full human being whom it is possible to like or dislike, because he is himself. All of this leads to a mood which is mainly despair, but one thinks of the few and clings to the hope.

The evidence of four years has not been comforting.

In the meantime, the unprovableness of his case is a source of anguish to the black man: failure of positive proof is a concomitant of increasing insight into motives and attitudes. To the accusation of being hypersensitive, the individual cannot reply convincingly. Inside, self-confidence is being destroyed. The constant necessity to ask oneself 'Is it because I am black or is it because I am, in fact, inferior and objectionable?' leads to a sapping of vital creative energy, and a withdrawal into introspection.

But is there not a kind of perception which relies, for its proof, on having been perceived?

3

The Weary Road to Whiteness and the Hasty Retreat into Nationalism

ELLIOTT BASTIEN

Trinidad

Elliott Bastien graduated with a B.Sc. (Hons.) in Chemical Engineering in 1963 and then attended a post-graduate course in Petroleum Production Engineering in Birmingham.

He wrote several articles for *Mermaid* (the literary magazine of the University of Birmingham) and is now collecting material for a book on Caribbean literature.

He returned to Trinidad in October 1964 to work in the Technical Civil Sevrice.

'THE greatest lie of our society', writes C. L. R. James, 'is that anywhere in these islands we have achieved racial harmony.' In the same vein he continues, 'In a book by a West Indian intended for West Indians I refuse to spend time disproving that racial harmony exists in the West Indies.' This may be justified, but the form of this essay does not permit the subject of racial harmony to be dismissed in quite so short a space (half of a page) as Mr. James uses. However, he does find it necessary to give a 'last word of warning' in the form of a postscript: 'Whatever the provocation, the subject demands a steady hand and a calm temper.' I shall try, along every step of the way, to keep these words before me.

To discuss racism in a West Indian context is to become hopelessly confused. One gets lost in a mass of contradictions,

and vacillation seems to be the rule of the day. This is because of
the peculiarly complex system of social stratification; a system
under which we live, and which is accepted by us, but never
examined. Never, that is, until we leave our island society and
are forced to face reality. And even so, the involvement was so
deep, and the brainwashing so subtle, that it is still difficult to
think straight and view the whole subject objectively. (Perhaps it
is not at all a good idea to be completely objective—even if this
were possible—in such matters.) An amazing degree of ambivalence is shown at all levels of the society. This can have its origin
in apathy, wide-eyed innocence—which is the same anyway—or
just downright hypocrisy.

Here is the calypsonian, the spokesman of the masses commenting on the racial situation in two calypsoes. They are both by the
Mighty Sparrow but I am not sure about the chronological order
which is unimportant as the time factor is not great.

From 'Leave the Dam Doctor':

> They makin' so much confusion
> 'Bout race riot in England.
> They should kick them from Scotland Yard,
> We have the same question in Trinidad.

And then an admirably well expressed verse that has a much more
than local significance.

> Well the way how things shapin' up,
> All this nigger business go' stop.
> I tell you soon in the West Indies
> Is please Mr. Nigger please.

Next comes 'Trinidad Carnival', and notice the popular national
myth being flattered. He says there is 'no colour question'.

> So jump and be merry
> Don' care how you black and ugly

because

> You could jump wid black
> You could jump wid white
> Jump until is twelve tonite.

There is a great deal of debate going on in West Indian circles about the interpretation of lyrics in the calypso, and especially about the danger of finding meanings that are not intended. Unconscious motivation is considered strictly taboo. This and more cannot take away from the splendid piece of sarcasm contained in those lines

> So jump and be merry
> Don' care how you black and ugly

—whether it be conscious or unconscious. Be merry Mr. Black and Ugly because 'you could jump wid white'. But only until 'twelve tonite'? Is Sparrow saying that racial harmony ends at 'twelve tonite'? I do not think, from the tone of the calypso, that this is what he means; but certainly from the construction of the verse this interpretation is valid. Unconscious motivation? This is the West Indian, then, contradicting himself at the normal level of awareness, but unconsciously adhering to the former opinion. It must be emphasized that this is at the root of the West Indian personality, an emotional state to which he has been conditioned by his environment. He really does believe in a strange way that racial discrimination at home exists and yet does not.

This phenomenon of the West Indian chameleon has to do with the fact that race prejudice and class prejudice are practically synonymous in the West Indies. The social structure is therefore of primary importance, and although its details may differ from island to island, the form of the structure in Trinidad, which I know best, may be used as a microcosm of the whole of the West Indies.

On the little island of Trinidad, history has deposited representatives of most of the races of the world who remain there up to this day. The white man came as the plantation owner and the black man as his slave. This relationship has its manifestation in the present time in the social stratification of the country. Lloyd Braithwaite points out that 'the social structure was clearly founded on an ascriptive-particularistic basis. It was based on the one hand on the positive evaluation of the white group and on the other, on a negative evaluation of the black group.' The indentured labourers, Chinese, Indians, and Portuguese, who were brought in after the abolition of slavery, 'therefore sought to differentiate themselves from the black group as much as possible'. In the beginning these immigrants were not considered to be part of the social system, or, if anything, to be on the lowest social scale. However, since they did not have to keep up with the standards of living in the island, they accumulated wealth and established a middle class. So that now the social ladder is white at the top and becomes progressively blacker further down the rungs. The further from Negro one is the higher up the ladder is one likely to be found.

What has been said above is only the rough sketch of a rather complicated masterpiece painted by Mr. Braithwaite and entitled *Social Stratification in Trinidad*. My sketch is by no means complete and lacks all the colour, the delicate shading, the subtle overlappings, the intricate interweaving and the fine perspective of the master. These must be painted in to portray the complex subject of race relations in the West Indies.

Trinidadians, and West Indians in general, have in V. S. Naipaul's phrase, 'a nice eye for shades of black'. The 'darker black' a man is, the less courteously he is treated, unless by some visible means he is recognized as one of high status; whereas the white man automatically receives deferential treatment. 'Nice hair', that is European or straight hair, is a considerable asset. 'European ideals of personal beauty have been taken over by the Trinidadian', but Indian or diluted Chinese features (that is mixed with another race, the Negro not excluded) are not unattractive, the texture of the hair approximating more closely to the European. Black men who have achieved a certain standard of wealth or education seek to improve their social standing even more by marrying a woman of lighter complexion. (White Trinidadians very seldom marry coloured Trinidadians.) This also ensures that their children will have a better start in life and is popularly known as 'putting milk in their coffee'. It is in this way that a middle class of coloured people has developed and it is not surprising that there are many spinsters among the educated and wealthy black women Some are forced to marry below their

D

status because of the reluctance of their menfolk to marry them.

Not only European standards of beauty have been adopted, but colonialism has also imposed European culture. And today Katrin Norris can write that the middle class 'went to great lengths to assimilate British characteristics'. Thus whereas in Europe it is the leisured class who perpetuate the culture, in the West Indies it is the lower class, as the middle class attempts to dissociate itself from art forms such as the calypso and the steel-band. This for the most part, though, is only superficial, and becomes blatantly obvious over the carnival period when race and class barriers are crushed by the bacchanalian crowds. But this only continues until Ash Wednesday ('twelve tonite'), when all the old barriers are carefully reconstructed and tint of skin becomes once more significant.

Tint-discrimination is the most appropriate term to apply to West Indian society. It applies among members of the same family. A well-known fact in the West Indies is that the offspring of coloured parents can vary quite widely in racial characteristics. So that it is possible in one family to have a son with European features, 'high brown' complexion and 'nice' hair and a daughter with negroid features, black skin and 'crinkly' hair. The son can often be invited to a party where the daughter is excluded, and permission by the parents to attend has been known to be given in such a case. This intermixture of races has led Mr. Naipaul to give the advice that 'in the West Indies . . . you must be absolutely sure of your company before you speak: you never know who is what, or more important who is related to what'.

In clubs too, the tint-discrimination line can pass through a family. The remarkable consistency in shade of the membership of clubs points to the existence of a very efficient colour 'sieve'. There is a club for the black middle class, black lower class, one for the 'high-brown' with European features, one for the brown with less pronounced European features, and of course, there are exclusively white clubs. These never refuse membership because of colour, but always on some other ground. In any case people nearly always go to a club where they are easily accepted. Also in existence are the Chinese Club, the Portuguese Club, and the

Indian Club. Most of these have cricket or football teams, and it is interesting to note that whereas most of the Trinidad representative team is coloured or black, the captain is invariably white.

This description of club life and sport in Trinidad is ten years old. Today very little of it has changed, although the West Indies has a black cricket captain for the first time in Frank Worrell. In fact the racial situation is changing only very slowly. The policeman is still as a rule aggressive towards the lower class (the black people), the Portuguese and Chinese are still looked upon as 'dirty shopkeepers', the Jews and Syrians (ironically classed together as 'Jew-men') as pedlars of clothing, the Indians as 'coolies' and cane-field workers, and the white man is still held in an aura of high esteem. Many West Indians will deny this, but although these distinctions are only superficial, they are still preserved in the family circle. The advertisements, carefully chosen, where 'black faces are normally used only . . . for things like bicycles and stout' reflect the mood of the people they serve to attract. Rivalry between the Indian and Negro has even been accentuated in recent years by the politicians.

Mr. James assures us that he can find no antagonism between the Indian and Negro, and that all classes of Indian and Negro have confirmed this. Also after a careful search he does not find that 'the black population has any ingrained hostility against whites'. Mr. Naipaul on the other hand is puzzled by Negro–Indian animosity, because 'at all levels they share the same language, the same ambitions . . . and increasingly the same pleasures'. 'Their interests don't clash.' He admits that there must have been a basic antagonism for the politicians to build on, and pessimistically prophesies a racial war. But alas! 'They despise one another by reference to the Whites; and the irony is that their antagonism should have reached its peak today when white prejudices cease to matter.' Both of these gentlemen are sincere and what is more both are correct. This is precisely the paradox of the West Indian situation.

But nowhere is there more duality (for want of a better word) than in matters of religion. 'God is a white man,' shouts Derek Walcott through the person of Afa in *The Sea at Dauphin*, 'the sky is his blue eyes, and his spit on Dauphin people is the sea.' And this is indeed brought home to the West Indian at a very early age, in the colour of the statues in the churches, in the fact that it is hard to conceive of a black pope. It is difficult for a Negro Roman Catholic to reconcile the teachings of the Church with the practice of racial discrimination by its pastors. The shock at discovering that segregation is practised in Roman Catholic churches in the southern United States is great indeed. In a Catholic college predominantly coloured, it is no accident that until recently, the Sixth Trinidad Sea Scouts (led by a priest) were all white, or that again until recently, the drama group (again led by a priest) was white to a man. To this latter statement, the aged priest-educator, a German, is reputed to have bluntly replied that Shakespeare did not write his plays for black people.

'I felt', says James Baldwin, 'that I was committing a crime in talking about the gentle Jesus, in telling them to reconcile themselves to their misery on earth in order to gain the crown of eternal life'; and the Negro position is neatly summarized. One of my African friends, himself a Christian, felt that the greatest evil to enter Africa was Christianity. The significance cannot be missed.

Religion, though, has had some effect in bringing the races together in the West Indies. But probably the greatest unifying force was, and is, the classroom, where all races mingle together. Any silly ideas of the intrinsic superiority of one race over another are destroyed by mere observation in the classroom and on the playing-fields. It is a lesson that is not forgotten in adult life, and non-white doctors and lawyers have many white people among their clientèle. From the very earliest stage, the white child comes into contact with black people, as black domestic servants are given complete control of the children of white families. Throughout his school career he meets and makes friends with coloured children, both sides realizing that after school hours they must be socially separate. The same applies to the professional relationships in later years.

It is in this way that the significant emotional experiences are shared by all races in the community. And although there is 'a natural segregation in residential districts, based upon economic positions without any legal restrictions as to purchase of property', which more or less tends 'to coincide neatly with ethnic divisions', the races are not all that far apart. Such considerations suggest that racial harmony exists to a certain extent. Another factor contributing to this belief is that the middle class does not frequent such places as clubs and restaurants, and is therefore not directly exposed to racial discrimination.

In matters concerning employment, however, it is difficult to overlook racial discrimination. Because the economy was con-controlled by metropolitan powers, European technicians and senior administrative staff were imported. White men thus filled the most important posts in the oil-fields in Trinidad and the banks were completely staffed by white people. This practice has ceased in the oil industry with the gaining of independence, and the banks have compromised by substituting 'high browns' and Chinese for white. As far as I know, no political pressure was applied for the passing of laws against racial discriminination in employment.

This economic division between the races has a great deal to do with the increased popularity of the Ras Tafarian movement in Jamaica. Katrin Norris maintains that 'Jamaica is virtually free from racial discrimination. . . . Discrimination if it can be called that is against the masses as a historically determined economic and cultural class, not as a racial group.' But the fact remains that the masses are black, and this has led to the formation of a new racist party in Back o' Wall in West Kingston, a stronghold of the Ras Tafarians. The Ras Tafarians are not unlike the Black Muslims in the United States. They consider themselves citizens of Ethiopia and as such outside the jurisdiction of the Jamaican Government. Following the words of their prophet Marcus Garvey—'Look to Africa when a black king shall be crowned, for deliverance is near'—and with the coronation of Haile Selassie (Ras Tafari) as Emperor of Ethiopia in 1930, they naturally looked upon Ethiopia as the fulfilment of the prophecy. They consider the white man their enemy, and the brown man his ally, and remain totally separated from them. However, the white man who tries to understand their viewpoint is considered an exception, and so too is the 'Black Man Judas'. This would seem to indicate that their 'racism' does not spring from any deep hatred of the white race. On the other hand, Vidia Naipaul believes that 'just as in England the Fascists frenziedly proclaim the racial attitudes of the majority who are scandalized only by the exhibitionism, so in Jamaica the Ras Tafarians express the basic racial attitudes of the majority of the black population.' This he emphasizes cannot be denied: and we wonder if it can!

The non-white population, including the coloured middle class, so preoccupied with their journey along 'the weary road to whiteness', have no time to examine this feeling in themselves. They will strenuously deny it. In fact if they do recognize it they will strive to suppress it. For all they aim at is admission to white society, the ultimate goal. This applies to all races in the West Indies with the probable exception of the lower classes who do not aim so high. Any obstacles in the West Indian's path to white acceptance are systematically crushed. His whole life pattern is geared to this one vital end. Lloyd Braithwaite draws from the theory of the 'jungle-world' to show how neatly the 'autocratic character' fits into the social structure of Trinidad. This is 'the tendency to regard most of all other human beings as challenging rivals who are either superior (and therefore to be feared, resented, bootlicked and admired) or inferior (and therefore to be scorned, humiliated and dominated).'

But anyone who knows the West Indies will beware of formulating rigid analyses. What appears to be and what is do not always coincide. Night falls quickly there, and the shadows lengthen and recede with the blinking of an eyelash. The shifting light can play fiendish tricks on the retina. The tide level is constantly changing. The atmosphere is conducive to vacillation and the effect on the personality cannot be overlooked. Slavery has taught the Negro to despise himself; it has imposed white civilization and destroyed belief in any other. Colonialism drew the remainder of the non-white population into this web of anomaly. The result of these backgrounds can only be a society where ambiguity is rampant. A few years ago Trinidad was known as the geologists' graveyard, and today the sociologists with their tidy system may well go there only to replace the geologists. The West Indian is a natural Existentialist.

This is the society that I was leaving that day in September 1960. 'Tous les visiteurs á terre s'il vous plait.' 'Todos los visitados a tierra por favor.' 'All visitors ashore please.' And what a relief it was to hear those words. The decks were in utter chaos.

There was an old relative who warned me of the dangers of not wearing proper underwear in the winter; my father insisting on my building up resistance with cod-liver oil; the fussy lady reminding me to take care of the parcel for her daughter whom I should go to see as soon as I landed (the daughter was in Ireland, I was to land at Southampton); a host of my father's friends, whom I knew, pointing out the ways of avoiding an early marriage, especially to a European; others, whom I did not know, advising me to carry my self-respect with me wherever I went so that I would always be accepted. There was a general confusion of advices, throughout which I nodded here, and smiled there, but not paying any particular attention to what was being said. I had been through it all so many times in the last week or two. Then suddenly, this old man, his paternal hand on my shoulder, with the air of authority that befits the aged, selected me out and commanded my attention. 'Son, never let anyone call you a Jamaican. If they do correct them sternly and immediately!' On the dock below the flag of the Federation was fluttering happily in the breeze, as the wet-eyed, whimpering women picked their way delicately down the gangplank; that old man, a Negro like myself, had never been to England. I was but twelve short days away.

'You can take the child out of the country,' quotes James Baldwin from his elders, 'but you can't take the country out of the child.' '. . . I found myself, willy-nilly, alchemized into an American the moment I touched French soil.' Both these sentences apply to the West Indian arriving in England, but in a far different way from their application to Mr. Baldwin. It is because the country cannot be taken out of the child (not immediately anyway), that the West Indian carries to England his criteria of social judgement. These of course are blatantly out of context to a certain relaxation in the presence of the whites because of the numerical majority of the coloured faces, when in England he is suddenly thrown into a minority group where 'dark brown' and 'high brown' or Indian and Negro have no real significance, his criteria must be modified. It is then that he is alchemized into a West Indian. Some students use the scarf to show that they are university people and not immigrants.

Trinidad, Barbados, Dominica. Where is that? What part of Africa?—The West Indian is quite sensitive about his African origin and through a thorough brainwashing is yet unable to think of Africa as anything but jungle and primitive peoples—No, the West Indies! Ah yes! You are a Jamaican. Well, sort of.

Students from the West Indies find this lack of knowledge of the Caribbean on the part of the English very surprising. Their entire formal education has been fashioned after that in an English school, and as a result, they feel that they know the English. They expect a certain reciprocity which in the majority of cases is non-existent. This is their first realization that they are different. Soon they are complimented on the standard of their English. Very good for a foreigner! The numerous parties for 'overseas students' are attempts to make them feel at home. Many white people go out of their way to impress upon the coloured student that the English hold no race prejudices. This patronizing, for that is what it is in effect, only serves to alienate the more sensitive. Of course I have seen the coloured student who is flattered by it and enjoys it. George Lamming is very harsh when he speaks of this type. 'They notice a cold stare, an enigmatic sneer, the built-in compliment which is used to praise and at the same time remind them who and what they are. But education has trained them in duplicity; their whole life becomes an experiment in double-think.' Obviously referring to the student again he adds, 'It is amazing what effort a certain type of West Indian will make in order to assure white friends that nothing has ever happened to him; that all his life in England has been a memorable participation in civilized pleasures.' They close their eyes to their experiences at the Saturday night hops. A girl who turns down their invitation to dance and gallops off immediately after with the next invitation, this time white. . . . They ignore the bus conductor who says 'thank you' until he gets to them, and the policeman who shows open annoyance at being asked directions. This type repeatedly denounces the immigrants and apologizes for their behaviour when no apology is required. 'There are different classes of black man, you know! When I see those scruffy Jamaicans, I am ashamed to be black and I keep far from them.' I have overheard many a West Indian student expressing this sentiment. No less obnoxious in our females is the derisive laughter invoked by the African.

The history which is responsible for this racial fear, this hatred of the blackness within ourselves, is the history of our colonialism. Colonialism, in Mr. Lamming's sense of the word, where Prospero has given Caliban the gift of language and created a state of affairs where Caliban is 'colonized by language and excluded by language'. 'It carried with it an unstated history of consequences, an unknown history of future intentions. This gift of language meant not English in particular, but speech and concept as a way, a method, a necessary avenue towards areas of the self which could not be reached in any other way.' 'It can relate to Law; and Law is more than a collection of rules for day-to-day conduct. Law is the expression of a particular spirit in a particular historic time and circumstances.' Richard Wright, in this way I believe, felt the 'painful contradiction in being at once a Westerner and a black man'.

The so-called new consciousness of the Negro is the coming-together of Negroes of different countries. They begin to realize a sense of unity in their relation to the white world. It is no more easy now for a Negro (Caribbean, African, or South American) to overlook the dreadful acts of brutality in the southern United States than it was for an English Jew to ignore the conditions in Hitler's Germany. To read in Hegel's *Philosophy of History*:

The Negro as already shown exhibits the natural man in his completely wild and untamed state. We must lay aside all thought of reverence and morality—all that we call feeling—if we would rightly comprehend him; there is nothing harmonious with humanity to be found in this type of character;

to observe the decision of *Wisden* to withdraw the status of 'Test Match' from their records and list all first-class cricket together, thereby neatly depriving the West Indian wicket-keeper Derek Murray of his newly gained world record (incidentally, it goes to Waite of South Africa); and after all this, to discuss racialism objectively requires a great miracle of perception and spiritual resilience. It is difficult for a Negro, whatever part of the world he may be from, not to identify himself with the Negro problem in South Africa or Alabama or anywhere else; and the amazing thing is that so many West Indians in England do not. (In the closed society of the West Indies itself, there is no such racial identification. This begins after leaving the West Indies and continues to exist on returning.)

The attitude to race problems in England cannot be isolated as an insular problem. It must be viewed as the Negro's right to acceptance as a man from a certain culture and not as an 'exceptional Negro' or an imitation white man. I have found that most Englishmen who have coloured friends accept them as one of their sort—we speak a common language—as an exception to the rest of the coloured folk. This is intended as a compliment. Here is a black man who has risen out of his group and embraced our standards. White men cannot seem to rid themselves of the idea that the coloured peoples need or want some intrinsic value which they, the whites, possess. The notion has been handed down from generation to generation and is proving difficult to dislodge now. The only blame we can attach to the youth is their reluctance to begin examining this tendency in themselves. The examination will be exceedingly difficult, but it can lead to a real change in their personal world, the surrender of a cherished dream. Will they begin this examination?

'Negroes know', Mr. Baldwin proclaims, 'how little most white people are prepared to implement their words with deeds, how little, when the chips are down, they are prepared to risk.

And this long history of moral evasion . . . has eroded whatever respect Negroes may once have felt for white people.' Whenever the question of South Africa comes up in the United Nations, Britain and the United States abstain. They continue to send arms to a white minority to suppress a black majority so that their investments may be safeguarded. At Birmingham University there was a great reluctance to impose a ban on South African goods in the Students' Union. Of course the intellectual arguments were put forward and one white student (a flat-mate of mine) even expressed surprise on learning that I felt so strongly about it. The Debating Society has also invited Mr. Max Mosley to speak there. Nowhere else in Birmingham is he allowed a platform! Of course the intellectual arguments were again put forward. Yet it is amongst these students that Mr. Baldwin looks for the racial solution. 'The student movement depends, at bottom, on an act of faith, an ability to see beneath the cruelty and hysteria and apathy of white people, their bafflement and essential decency. It demands a perpetually cultivated spiritual resilience for the bulk of the evidence contradicts the vision.' I know that many people will say that James Baldwin is discussing the American situation and that what he says does not apply in England. All I can say to them is, 'Remember Notting Hill. People said that it could not happen. It is still happening in the streets at night. Read the newspapers.'

Lewis Chester, in the *Sunday Times*, can write that Smethwick 'is a town where most lounge bars exclude "coloureds" and some of the barbers refuse to cut immigrant hair ("It's too crinkly, you see")'. Mr. Patrick Gordon Walker, the Labour 'Shadow' Foreign Secretary, has narrowed his majority because of his opposition to the Commonwealth Immigrants Act. The Secretary of the British Indian Workers' Association has taken the unprecedented step of advising all Indians to vote anti-Tory, because he describes the housing proposal as 'the latest in a long series of racialist proposals made by the Tories for political ends'. Mr. Peter Griffiths, the personal object of the Secretary's scorn, admits he is not 'an integration man'. 'I think more in terms of peaceful co-existence. After all the Indians are no more in favour of mixed marriages than we are.' This is particularly important, not because Mr. Griffith is leader of the Conservative group, but because he is headmaster of a junior school. Labour members have also resigned in disapproval of the integration policy. 'One former Labour councillor now runs a "Whites only" youth group. The well-appointed Labour Club run independently of the constituency has no coloured members.'

At Sheffield, I think, there was a case reported in the newspaper of a policeman who framed a Jamaican because he was 'going with' a white girl. He was caught. Many incidents have been related to me of policemen arresting coloured men and planting 'weed' in their pockets. It is rare that the accused can prove their innocence in the light of the statements of the policeman (usually two) and even so the process is too costly for most to afford. Whether these incidents are factual or not, most West Indians believe them to be, and now hold little trust in the British police. Many had first-hand knowledge of police behaviour during the Notting Hill riots, and are no longer colour-blind where the law is concerned.

Coloured people are victimized in England in numerous ways from rent to car insurance. The Rachmanesque landlords capitalize by raising the rent and dividing up the rooms. Upkeep is dispensed with; and people still wonder why black neighbourhoods are so shabby. If the coloured peoples protest or take any group action, the whites look for outside agitators—Communists or others. They thereby imply that the coloured peoples cannot act on their own initiative; they have to be manipulated. No thought is given to the utter fear with which so many immigrants live; fear of being thrown on to the cold streets, sometimes with young families, at a moment's notice. Police aid they do not even bother to seek. Yet the sociologists go there and come out armed with their statistics, thinking that they have discovered something of the people. So many are unemployed, so many have illegitimate children, so many have got into trouble with the law (doubtful figures most believe); and what does that say about the people? Does it say how the less physically equipped of us (including myself) dread to walk alone in the streets at night?

In fact most English people do not want to know about West Indians. They like to hold on to their myths. The calypso-singer, or the guitar-player, or the limbo dancer, or the cricketer, that is the West Indian. He is the man whom white children and drunken 'bums' can beg for money without shame for he has no personality, no value of money. Write a poem or a novel and they applaud this strange phenomenon loudly without bothering to look at the quality. George Lamming tells us how maddened he was to realize that the literary critics, and Kingsley Amis in particular, did not, or rather could not, consider the West Indian novel as a subject for serious discussion. The old fear of the sexual potency of the black man is still there, as strong as ever, to complicate matters still further. To walk through the streets with a white girl at your side is to run the gauntlet of staring white faces. Faces that can see one reason and one only for that white girl being with you—'She couldn't possibly be "decent".' Ignorance must be eradicated from both sides before racial harmony can become a possibility.

Jean-Paul Sartre in *The Reprieve* expresses most aptly the feelings of the West Indian.

It isn't good for a man to live on other man's territory, it is very hard to bear; he is grudged the bread he eats. And their suspicion—that supremely ... [English] suspicion of us! When I get back to ... [The West Indies] this is the vision I shall have of ... [England]: a long dark staircase, a bell, a door half-opened—'What do you want?'—and then shut again. . . . What I find hardest to bear is to be a charge on others. Especially when they make you feel it so cruelly.

('England', 'English' and 'the West Indies' have been substituted for 'France', 'French' and 'Vienna' respectively.)

In this atmosphere then, it is not strange that many West Indians in England give birth to a Caribbean nationalism. With *négritude* some even seek to encompass much wider areas. Is this a hasty retreat into nationalism? Is it because of the frustrations encountered in England along the weary road to whiteness? Many of our people attain the age of maturity, both physically and intellectually, in this country. This maturity brings with it the awareness of the contradiction involved in being a black

Westerner, especially in a minority group in a white country. The tendency to discard the secondhand culture and religion is natural. To replace them, a national culture, which existed all the time, is now cultivated and proudly displayed. The castle is restored to its rightful place. (Mr. Lamming found it necessary to make this restoration. Derek Walcott used the phrase 'in the castle of *your* skin' in describing white people in one of his poems. Mr. Lamming took the phrase *In the Castle of* My *Skin*, the title of one of his novels, to refer to the black man.) But how easily can all these years of British-type education be thrown off and prevented from affecting our way of seeing?

'A truly Jamaican nationalist with education', answers Katrin Norris, 'is rare. After ten or fourteen years of striving to become British, the product of such an education system must be convinced that "British is Best" and consequently the intellectual leadership of Jamaica is from its earliest days emasculated of the independent spirit and vigour which could only come from a heartfelt national consciousness and pride.' The task of our youth, then, is to begin to realize that all that is British is not best; and the task of our Governments is to replace the present educational system with one more appropriate. Must the product of the new system believe that 'West Indian is Best'? Must the pendulum swing from one extreme to the other before settling at the centre?

4

The Transition from
'Light Skinned' to 'Coloured'

PATRICIA MADOO

Trinidad

Patricia Madoo was born in 1940, in Trinidad. She left in 1960 to read Modern History at St. Anne's College, Oxford. In 1963 she obtained an Honours B.A. and is now studying at the Department of Social and Administrative Studies, Oxford, for the Diploma in Public and Social Administration. She hopes eventually to obtain an M.A. in Sociology.*

THE light-coloured West Indian student, on arrival in Britain, if he has despite his education remained typical of his class, seems to share the colour prejudice of the white people among whom he has come to live. Yet in essence this prejudice is different, for it is based on the snobbery of his class, not on an unreasoning antipathy to blackness. He regards himself as more white than black, more like the English than like the black men from his own or any other country: he expects both English and black men to recognize this fact. To him the Indian is a strange, rather frightening creature, associated unconsciously with the 'coolies' who work on the plantations at home. The African is alien and exotic, very much nearer the primitive than he is. The black West Indian he links automatically with the rough lower classes of his own country—unless by his education and ability he can prove otherwise. The Englishman, that exalted being who has often been so

* We are publishing the second part of Miss Madoo's essay. The first part contains a description of various aspects of the colour problem in Trinidad. Similar descriptions will be found in other essays from the West Indies included in this book.

kind at home and with whom he feels so much in common, he sees quite trustingly as a potential friend and soul-mate, the last barriers having gone down when he came to England to study. In this attitude the West Indian student is surely unique among coloured students coming to England to study.

Some people never alter this attitude. They may be lucky in their contacts or insensitive in their assessment of the reaction to themselves, but they experience no great disillusionment. They can be met years later, speaking with flawless English accents, dressed in perfect English turnouts, surrounded by a group of English friends, quite possibly married to English people. They may return home to dazzle relatives with tales of their social triumph and to lament the lost glories of student days in England: or they may never return. Yet these types are a minority.

For the average student the beginning of the disillusionment comes almost immediately. Perhaps the first blow will come with his quite casual observations in the port of disembarkation and in the railway stations through which he passes on his way to the university town. Here he sees white men, English men, doing menial jobs. With part of his mind he had known this all along. He had been told it, he had read it, he had reasoned it out. But only now and only gradually does the full realization come that the English too are divided into classes, that their lowest classes, though white, are no different from the black lower classes at home. He becomes as adept as the English at picking out class by accent and educational history.

The consequences are twofold, and both operate in reshaping his attitude to the colour problem. As has been shown earlier, the light-coloured West Indian student's colour prejudice is little more than his class snobbery. The basis of this snobbery is the belief that whiteness denotes high social status. This basis is now destroyed. Class differences operate within the white group, within the English society which had hitherto been to him the pinnacle of social success. He realizes that many of the English people at home who deigned to be friendly, and even more of those who could not be bothered, were in fact, in their own country, lower down their own social ladder than he was on his.

This is a bewildering reversal of his scale of values. With part of his mind he looks much more critically at the system of white superiority exercised in his own island. This happens at the same time as his acceptance of all those ideas against class inequalities so popular in universities. With another part of his mind, however, he dimly sees another answer to his problem. If he can mix freely with English circles similar to those in which he moved at home then in an odd way everything will be as it was before. He can prove his right to his position in his own society by gaining recognition from the concomitant social group in England.

It is in this quest for acceptance, not for a formal acknowledge-ment of equality, but for an unconscious acceptance which shows that equality exists, that the West Indian student comes into contact with the English brand of colour prejudice. This operates on the assumption that a man by being coloured is different in a number of ways, apart from the degree of pigmentation, from anyone who is white. For many English the belief in this differ-ence is enough. Their age-long insularity comes into operation. They remain completely aloof, completely indifferent to the coloured student sitting or standing or reading next to them. For the coloured student contact with these is impossible. There are others who are prepared to be more friendly, less narrow. They hold that the coloured person although different is interesting as well. It is from these that the West Indian student hears the statement of difference reiterated over and over again, though seldom in precise terms. Together with this he learns of the English belief that all coloured people, while different from the English, have a great deal in common with each other. In fact there is an accepted stereotype of the coloured person, altered slightly for a coloured student, which is applied automatically to every dark face encountered.

With all these obstacles operating to prevent the Englishman from seeing the coloured individual as an individual and not as a type, the coloured student can never make the break-through to that position of unconscious acceptance which alone can satisfy his urge for equality. He finds himself invited to tea parties always to find that they are 'international' tea parties and that another coloured person has been invited with whom, it is expected, he will be able to relax. He is asked 'How long have you been speaking English?' or 'When did you become a Christian?' He is told 'All you people are as alike as peas', or 'You are all so gay', or (by a tutor) 'It is amazing that you can grasp so easily an essentially English concept.' All this is an enormous blow to the self-confidence of the light-coloured student who has been brought up in the belief that he differs obviously from other coloured people, being 'almost English' both in appearance and upbringing. He takes the reiteration of difference as a rejection. He has discovered that the Englishman is as intensely conscious of colour as he himself is of shade differences at home. Should he holiday on the Continent in one of the poorer countries he will find the English attitude underlined more clearly by contrast. He finds that in the country he is visiting, while the fact that his skin is brown is observed, it is given little more meaning than the fact that his eyes too are brown. In England this never happens. The brown or black face registers immediately, calling into action a whole series of acquired attitudes. Eventually the student comes to watch for this process in operation every time he meets a stranger. He waits expectantly for the result: either the friendly smile to 'the stranger in our midst' or that curious sliding away of the eyes which is the reaction of those who maintain the attitude of indifference.

The realization of this rejection is a cumulative one. It is like being asked to sit at the back of a bus. Gradually the efforts to be absorbed into English circles cease. Equally slowly a feeling of bitterness grows. Evidence of active colour prejudice is easily accepted and subjectively applied. Stories of black people refused accommodation, scrawled sentences in the Underground saying 'Nigger leave our girls alone', accounts by acquaintances who were chased during the race riots, all are emotionally received as a direct insult to oneself and one's kind. Personal experience of incidents of prejudice—a newspaper agent who flatly and without reason refuses to accept an order for a daily paper, the frosty reception by the parents of a friend who has long hesitated over the introduction, the loud, grinning conversation about 'a black

Jamaican bitch' accepting vast sums of National Assistance, from a group fully aware of one's presence at the next table—all these, which might in other circumstances have been brushed off as the foolish behaviour of a few individuals, seem instead just extreme examples of a national attitude. Just at the critical moment for a student of the last four years comes the Immigration Act. This is followed by the actual experience of it when next he returns from a holiday abroad. He has the humiliating experience of leaving his student group to pass through the doorway labelled 'Commonwealth and Irish citizens only', there to have an encounter with the officials nasty enough to make him wonder what happens to the coloured people who are really trying to come in to work. Then come the stories of deportation under the Act. The student is convinced that national prejudice has received official sanction.

The result of all this is an almost complete withdrawal—intellectual and emotional—from the English. He accepts their view that he is different from them but similar to all coloured people. He intensifies the degree of his contact with other West Indians. He clings eagerly to the idea that he shares in a distinctive West Indian culture, separate from the English culture in which, the English have implied, he has no part. In the radical circles which are West Indian student circles in Britain he hears expounded the historical causes of his own family's shade prejudice, he hears the whole social structure operating on this principle condemned and rejected. As part of his withdrawal from all things white he too rejects the system. Further, he accepts the social segregation imposed on him by the English: he joins all the 'International Clubs' and 'Commonwealth Clubs' and 'Overseas Students' Clubs', he makes friends with coloured people from other countries. Partly because of his mood, partly because of the actuality, he discovers an affinity with them whose existence, on his arrival in England, he would never have accepted. One day he reads of some outrage in South Africa or the southern U.S.A.: by his unexpectedly intense fury and sorrow he realizes that a transformation has occurred. He has become a black man, taking his side in the array of black versus white.

After this realization has been made most of the tension goes out of the student's attitude. Sure of the fundamentals—what he is and where he stands—he can afford to relax on details. Over the years of further study he tests his attitude to coloured people and finds that it holds good, and that it is accepted by them. He can take a new interest in England and things English—the interest of a visitor living for a period of years in a foreign country. He discovers that once he too accepts the first premise that he is different, it is possible to form real friendships with a few English people. He may even discover a genuine liking for whole elements in British society: the left-orientated group of students, or the lively working and lower-middle classes. He realizes that, in one sense, his personal experience of real unpleasantness was just caused by the action of a few foolish individuals who would have embarrassed the majority of English people as much as they enraged him. Yet nothing in these years occurs to disprove his earlier experience of the basic English inability to accept coloured individuals unreservedly. Nothing occurs to shake his conviction that he can never lose himself completely among these strange, cold, white people. He belongs on the other side of the fence. He will have to return home.

It might be wondered how this altered being will be able to live in his own peculiar society. Should he have the opportunity to go home on holiday during his studies he will have a preview of his future life there. He will realize that a few changes are occurring: that a large number of graduates have returned; that his country, by obtaining political independence, has experienced a breakdown of shade barriers in politics and in the personnel of the administration and of education. All this will make it possible for him to have friends who share his views, and fields of activity where his attitudes will not immediately cause conflict. Yet he finds his family—in the extended sense in which the word can be used in the West Indies—and their friends exactly as he left them. Their snobbery and prejudices still operate. Only the student is different. His attitude is one of detachment and of a general amusement at the comic-opera qualities of a small island's society. He attempts to fulfil his family obligations, but remains aloof from the social attitudes which these obligations hitherto involved. The distance put between him and his family by several years' separation makes this aloofness a practical possibility. Yet he realizes that his experiences in England while forcing him to break down old barriers have erected a few new ones. The complete relaxation among family and former friends, a relaxation based on a general acceptance of their common place in the social system, can never again come about. The light-coloured graduate has become an outcast, though a voluntary outcast, in his own society. Although shade differences no longer mean anything to him or to his new friends, none of them can be unaware of the fact that they do exist, living as they do in a society which concentrates so hard on the differences. For a long time he will be regarded as a bit of a rarity whose presence will have to be accepted in the largely dark-coloured graduate circle in which he moves. For the rest of his life he will be thought 'odd' by his family and former friends, though the prestige accruing to him as a graduate will in part make up for this oddity.

Before concluding I must comment on a foreseeable criticism of this essay by other coloured people, who may argue that my description of English colour attitudes is too kind, that they, from their own experience, know of a more virulent form of prejudice. The answer is that although I will not deny the existence of this prejudice I have not myself experienced it. This may be because I have spent most of my time in England in a small university town, not in a large metropolis where feeling is possibly less restrained; or it may be that my light colour has in fact shielded me from more severe experiences. What I myself argue is that the 'friendliness to the stranger' attitude, although very much in evidence in my university town, is itself the product of the liberal tradition which the university generates. The other attitude, the belief in the difference of coloured people and the indifference to them which this belief calls forth, is very probably the attitude of the majority in the country at large. That this attitude is potentially dangerous I believe strongly enough to satisfy anyone who might think me lukewarm about the English attitude to colour.

The whole experience of living in England, though at first

almost traumatic, is of extreme value for the West Indian student, particularly the light-coloured student. I have no knowledge of what the experience does for the African or Indian, but I cannot help feeling that the consequences for the light-coloured West Indian student are more wide ranging. He has removed an incipient white-type colour prejudice; he has his position as a member of one of the coloured races clearly outlined for the first time; he has a whole series of class prejudices overturned; he has the colonial myth of his almost-British personality completely destroyed. In the end realization of this makes it impossible for him to be bitter about his stay in England. The English have at last rendered him a service.

5

Some Contexts of Blackness

SILLATY K. DABO

Sierra Leone

Sillaty K. Dabo was born in 1937 at Gboyama in the Bo District, Sierra Leone, into a large Muslim family. He studied Arabic for a few years. He hopes to join the Education Department on return to Sierra Leone at the end of his studies here. For two years he was in France, at the Sorbonne and the University of Montpellier. At present he is doing post-graduate work in Oxford in the field of comparative literature.

LOOKING back now, six years after the incident, it seems as if I first considered the problems of discrimination when locked up in Fly's room that Friday night.

'But oh dear! Why don't you listen to me, Hunmoi? You must try to understand my position. As. . . .'

Those were his last words when, on hearing the sound of footsteps on the stairs, he pushed me into the dark room, bolting the door instantly. The window was open because I could feel the fresh air.

I did nothing for the first five minutes. I stood still, there, in the middle of the room, doing nothing until my eyes gradually got used to the darkness. Then I heard the silvery laughter of Mrs. Edwards, ringing high above even the coarse voice of A. H., her husband. I was too furious and restless. It had never occurred to me that Fly, too, could ever deceive me. But perhaps deceive is not the right word. So much the worse for that! In any case this was a great disappointment for me. It was not that I had expected Fly to behave very differently from other men, particularly other white men.

Take the case of old Father Davis, of the Roman Catholic School at Mbékor, the Poor Man! Not that I really liked him or the Headmaster at the time. In fact if anything, I think I hated them both, though I must confess that theirs was a difficult task. How I would have liked to see them carry out their threats. I wonder whoever gave these two the brilliant idea of compelling Muslims to go to church on Sundays or, failing this, to give them half-a-dozen lashes every Monday morning? Of course it seemed then a clever solution (a very easy and pleasant one for the African Headmaster, who could be seen every Monday morning with a list of absentees from Sunday School, and holding in his left hand, TERROR, his long whip) to the problem of the propagation of Christianity in the middle of the Dark Continent.

I don't suppose the blame was one-sided. My parents too should share some of it. I do not think that I should have become a Christian if Dad had let me go to church on Sundays. He would have probably allowed me to go, but I don't believe some of the other members of the family would have approved of this. However, not satisfied with the six lashes they gave us every Monday morning, our two friends hit upon a more brilliant idea. I am almost certain this was the Headmaster's idea: all Muslims were going to be dismissed from the school, and none would be admitted in future unless they became converts!

How I wish they had consulted me. It never occurred to them that Dad would take them on their word, or that there was a fairly large number of Muslims in the school. The only other probability is that they were just making an empty threat to see whether our parents could be frightened and brought to their knees. Anyway, we stayed at home for a day or two, and both the threat and corporal punishment were withdrawn. I was very grateful. I must point out also that it is most unlikely that Dad would have allowed any of the children from the neighbouring villages, who were staying in our compound, to go to church on Sundays. If they had, he would have probably punished them or sent them away from the compound. The need did not arise, however, because their parents had previously been converted to Islam by my father.

None of these things would have made me detest Father Davis and the Headmaster if they had not gone to extremes in their hatred of Muslims, and of my family in particular. My brother and some friends were walking a long distance on the motor road when a van came up the road. Who else could be the occupants but Father Davis, the Headmaster, and another Reverend Father? They gave a lift to all but my brother. I was very angry when I heard this, and my brother certainly dramatized the situation a little.

Now that I know the reasons for what seemed to be a total lack of generosity, I have long since modified my views. It happened that two days before, Father Davis and the Headmaster (from now on referred to as H. M.) had called on Dad asking to be allowed to build a school in another village in the District. Dad seems to have been willing to grant them permission but promised to discuss the matter over with my brother. Father Davis and the H. M. were to return the following morning. The next day Dad did not give them permission to build the school. The permit was given to the Methodist Mission, where the question of church services was never seriously discussed.

I think this was one of the many reasons why Father Davis and his party did not give a lift to my brother. I wonder who is to blame? None of them forgave the other when he should have. I think they were both too strict, and this, in my view, is probably not in the interest of any of the great religions they stand for. One must of course allow for the spirit of the age and environment, and in the middle of the Dark Continent at the time, this attitude on the part of each is understandable.

But as I was saying before this religious incident, I was really perturbed by the fact that Fly had to shut me up in his room simply because A. H. and his wife were coming to see him! Why he should have to do this was beyond my understanding, and to hear him pleading with me to 'try to understand his position' only aggravated an already bad situation. Fly was only a few years my senior, though he had already got his first degree a few years before I was to leave for Britain for further studies.

I had met him at my father's only eight months before, but,

until that Friday night, it seemed as though we had known each other for years. He was very kind, and I looked on him as a personal friend. As a young man just waiting to proceed to Britain, I used to take him home with me, in his car, of course. My parents liked him too. He was so simple! I used to go to dances with him. I would introduce him to friends and acquaintances, males and females, who thought highly of him too. Why, then, should he behave the way he did that evening?

The answer seems to be that A. H. who had been in another part of Africa for a much longer time than Fly, and had just been posted to our territory a few months after his former territory had attained independence, did not quite like the idea of his deputy's going about with Africans. 'I have lived in Africa much longer than yourself. I know these people. . . . Mm. . . . Yes, I know them, I know them only too well. . . . You remember the old saying, that familiarity breeds contempt?'

I could imagine him saying such things, and I must say that there is always some truth in these sayings, even when they come from men like A. H. In the case of Fly and myself, however, I know that on no account did I try to take undue advantage of his kindness. It is not that I did not like men of the generation of A. H. In fact some of his contemporaries rendered more services to Africa than some of us Africans would probably ever be able to give. Another point is that if A. H. and I had met at Dad's, Fly would not have been reluctantly compelled to subject me to such a disgrace. Anyway, in spite of the fact that conditions were changing rapidly everywhere in the world, including even Africa, A. H. would much rather have Fly and other young junior officers continue to maintain formalities—even decadent and destructive ones—in Africa. They had to toe the line or fall out. Poor Fly! I don't think I have really quite forgiven him ever since, though we are still great friends. I feel instinctively that he should have put up a stronger attitude to meet the threats from A. H.

I do not in fact think that A. H. would have put up much resistance anyway. For one thing, he might just have been pretending to be tough; for another, he was still new in the place and he would certainly need much co-operation from Fly. Besides, if I had been with my father at Fly's at the time of A. H.'s visit, I should never have been locked up in a room. Nor do I think that, except for his stubborn adherence to decadent formalities, A. H. was in fact a very bad man. We met a few days later, at George's, the English teacher. This being neutral ground (for most European teachers in Africa, apart from South Africa, are friendly with the pupils) we actually got on fairly well after we had been introduced. I wish he could have been less paternalistic though!

The atmosphere in Britain was so different when I arrived late one summer afternoon. The Hall of Residence was so terribly quiet. Most of the students were still on holiday. Only one or two had come a few days before. I sat alone in my room, feeling hopelessly lonely and lost, when, at about half-past six at night, a gentleman came to my room to say dinner was ready and invited me to follow him.

There was very little conversation at table. I was actually deceived when, on telling him from where I came, my friend said: 'Oh yes, I see.' Well, I thought, he really knew the place, or its exact position on a map of Africa. It was long afterwards that I came to know that he didn't. However, after dinner my friend took me round the grounds, and later invited me to supper, asking me what classical or pop records I would like to listen to. Here too, we didn't have much conversation. Yet my friend was very kind, in his own way.

It was very embarrassing for me the first day we reopened. None of my classmates would sit in the same row with me. This made me stand out all the more clearly. I was the only African in the Department. When some days later I got to know a few people, I began to understand that they had stayed away because they felt shy, some even saying that they were not sure what my reaction would have been if they had approached me earlier! It was a pity that even when I had made a fairly good start, some of those who got fewer marks than myself took refuge in saying that since I was not English and happened to get better marks than themselves, it was obviously because my essays were not marked on the same standard. I am sure some of these friends were joking, and I hope I am right in this.

I was astonished when my friend and his girl friend, who had invited me to a dance in the country, began to apologize, on the way to the place, because they felt I might be refused several times! My reply was that I had already prepared myself for everything the day I left home, and begged them not to bother with such silly things. Well, things were a trifle more difficult than I had expected, at least from the start. In the first place I was the first coloured man they had seen in that hall for years, and there was much curiosity as we entered. But that was not all. The first six girls I asked for a dance refused, in a rather hypocritical, if polite manner; that is, with a quick smile and a 'no, thank you'. You can never imagine how demoralizing this could be even for a young pretender claiming to be a stoic. Because of the rather odd way in which these girls sit together, you would have no choice but continue to go down the line. Those who had already refused would now be busy either devouring you with their eyes or discussing you!

I was really ashamed as I felt all eyes on me. I was perspiring fast. Luckily I got my reward. The seventh girl agreed to dance with me. I still do not know whether it was her genuine desire to dance with me or she was led to this decision through a sense of pity! Anyway the piece played at the time was a quick-step which, by chance, I could do perfectly. Bravo, and thanks to that girl! After that even those of her friends who had refused me previously were quite willing to, and did dance with me.

Personally I hate rushing to conclusions, and I don't like sweeping generalizations either. Were the girls in the first place afraid to dance with me because of public opinion? The public being the young men crowded at the bar, drinking, chatting, and perhaps watching the girls dancing among themselves? Were they not sure whether the African they saw before them was, in spite of his smart appearance, exactly like the ones they had read about in their simplified, romantic, exotic readers? Was he the living savage himself? How could they be sure that this man, the first coloured man they have seen, in fact, knew how to dance? Did they want to be absolutely sure of this before staking their own self-respect? Since he would surely be going back the same night, was it worth while for a girl hoping to be married, to accept an invitation for a dance from one who, even if she could like him, was not going to marry her anyway? Would she not stand to lose much by this, with all the young men looking on? These were probably some of the questions the girls I asked for a dance that evening were asking themselves, and which others I would be asking in the future would possibly have to ask themselves.

On the other hand this provided me with sufficient experience. The patterns change according to the locality, whether one is in a university town or not, or in an industrial city or in a small town. Much would probably depend also on the personality of the individual. I should point out, however, that it would be naïve to ascribe incidents of the kind described above to colour prejudice; certainly there is the colour problem involved. But it is also true that I was refused dances by African girls even before I came to Europe, that I have been refused by them here a number of times, and, not being particularly a ladies' man, I know I would be refused by some more in the future, both here and in Africa. I have even taken some European friends to African dances here where they could hardly get a single dance.

What I quite frankly dislike in discussing the colour problem is hypocrisy. It is not uncommon to meet children walking with their parents on the street, and who, on seeing an African, point to him or her saying, 'Mum (or Daddy), look at that Blackman', or, very rarely 'Nigger'. Quite often the parent feels embarrassed, draws the child away with such statements as 'Don't be rude to the gentleman (or lady).' Well, children often use these expressions without realizing what their effects would be. And what about that? I am black and I am a Negro or Nigger depending on what the child hears from home or from friends. The fact that it points at me is not particularly strange. I have seen children run away in my village when a European approaches. The difference is that as opposed to his position in my village, where he is highly respected, here in Europe, I am rather generally regarded as an inferior being, quite often because of sheer ignorance, but occasionally because of the kind of education we have been given, both Africans and Europeans. The psychological effects of this are considerable and are not easy to destroy.

Whenever I cross the Channel, I cannot help feeling the change of atmosphere. 'Frère, je me sens presque comme si j'étais chez moi,' an African student from Congo (ex-Belgian) once told me in Paris. He had been to Geneva, Bonn and Rome, where, he complained, people were always staring at him. In Paris, he felt quite at home, and this, in spite of the fact that he had been there for less than twelve hours. Was this probably because he could speak French?

Some English friends have often asked me why Africans in France look much happier than those in England. I do not know whether they have actually conducted a research into this, but I personally do not know the answer. Probably it lies in the study of the French way of life, which is not the subject of this essay. John Hatch says in his book *Africa Today—and Tomorrow* in his discussion on Algeria: 'Social integration, however, hardly exists except that the French settlers are more subtle than their British counterparts in patronizing the handful of educated Arabs.' In his autobiography, Dr. Nkrumah, then Prime Minister of the Gold Coast (now Ghana) described his visit to the then French Cameroons (now part of the Republic of Cameroun) in 1952 as follows: 'One thing that I remember very vividly about the occasion—probably because it was the first time that I have ever seen it happen in any colony—was the way all the workers, both European and African, climbed into the waiting lorries when the lunch buzzer sounded. This complete disregard of colour on the part of the European workers greatly impressed me.'

These quotations need no comments for the time being. We may come to them later. I still remember vividly the first reaction of my French student friend with whom I stayed at a hostel for a year. The hostel was in fact a Jesuit centre, and I was admitted there after I had already told them that I was a Muslim. They were very kind to me, even giving me a small carpet for my prayers. They were singularly tolerant compared with the

Catholic school I went to in Africa. Why this difference in principles?

As soon as we had been introduced, my friend helped me with my luggage, took me to the refectory, and told me, *en route*, practically everything about himself! It was as though we had known each other for years. Incidentally, however, he did not invite me to his room for a very long time. We usually always met in the refectory or in one of the cafés near the hostel.

Later on, I got to know a very kind French family. They invited me to dinner every week, and I always received a small note informing me about the time and date. Even when I became just one of the family, I don't remember ever walking into their house unannounced.

Another African student who had spent nearly six years in that particular place confessed that he had never been invited by any family. He concluded that the French were not very kind to African students (he probably meant African students and the French in this place). I tried to suggest that the French, particularly those in the South, do not normally entertain at home, as opposed to the idea of the Englishman and his castle, and that much of the social life anyway was spent outside, in cafés, etc. My friend was not convinced. I felt that it was probably much easier to know English families and to get invited to their homes than French families. In spite of this, I had a feeling that one would probably feel much more at home in France than in England. This depends of course on the character and personality of the individuals concerned. I wonder whether this sort of situation would help in any way my English friends who wanted to know why French-speaking Africans in France seem much happier than English-speaking Africans in Britain. Do they imbibe more of French culture, or do they understand the French better than their counterparts in England? To the first question the answer would possibly be yes, but the second question is a little more difficult, and I have no answer to it myself. But perhaps this point would be better understood from this remark by William Conton, the author of the book *The African*, in which he is discussing this problem:

It is perhaps a pity that the British, with their traditional reserve, were the most successful of African imperial powers. For reservation shown to a once-subject people is at once interpreted as prejudice. Two pairs of eyes meet across a ship's lounge or smoking room: a copy of *The Times* is promptly interposed across the line of vision by the Briton, and the African sucks his teeth and curses him in his heart. In fact, of course, the Briton would have made exactly the same gesture if his eyes had met almost any other strange ones. And so gestures create attitudes, and attitudes in turn give colour to gestures, and the waters are soon poisoned almost beyond cleansing.

One could continue to give his personal experiences about the colour problem before and after his arrival in the United Kingdom. But if we tried to put some order into all the experiences described above, it seems that they would tend to fall roughly into five categories, namely: *religious*, as shown in the episodes in which the Catholic priest and my family are involved. These were clearly non-racial issues, because as I tried to point out, Dad would have been ready to punish anybody in our compound who went to church on Sundays. Likewise, the Catholic priest and the H. M. did not whip all African children in the school every Monday morning. Only those who refused to go to church. When Dad refused to allow the Catholics to build another school in the District, he did not give it to Africans, but to another European Mission, though then there was no obligation on the part of the children to go to church on Sundays.

The incident concerning Fly, A. H., and myself was purely a *social* problem. The proof that this is so could be seen from the fact that if my Dad had been present at the time, I would not have been shut up in a room. The fact that A. H. and I met at George's a few days later and that I was never locked up supports this view.

Cultural: the different reactions I had from meeting my two student friends, one English and the other French, and my own experience in living in these two countries show that there were cultural differences between my friends and myself, on the one hand, and also between the two of them on the other.

Psychological: the episode at the dance is a psychological one in the sense that these girls had been given a certain image of the African and of his way of life. We also saw a similar situation gaining ground in the incident in which a child and its mother were involved. If allowed to continue unchecked, it would become more difficult at a later stage in life, to efface such distorted pictures from the subconscious.

Historical: this is an important factor. It shows the degree of development of Africa and the African at the time of the first contact between the European and the African. The European, relying on his technological superiority, conquered the almost defenceless African and made him into his servant. With the discovery of the New World and the subsequent slave trade, the relationship was modified to suit the new situation. This was the kind of image which the colonial powers gave of the African, and it has continued, with slight modifications, and in spite of political independence, to the present day. If anything needs immediate changing, so as to build a new world based on freedom, equality and fraternity among the peoples of the world, it is this image which must be changed.

Of course it would be wrong to pretend that economic, historical and all the other differences referred to above, exist only between peoples of different races. Even within the same nations, in Britain, for instance, there are tremendous differences in the standard of living and education of the citizens. The economic disparities are being gradually narrowed down. However, it is when such conflicts come from a racially conditioned class system that they will serve to aggravate an already strained situation. The fear of the ruling minority of being swamped by the suffering masses is matched by the almost implacable antagonism and detestation of the former by the latter.

Cases of this kind of economic conflict are many in history. The real test of the sincerity of the noble ideals of the ruling powers would not come until there emerged a sufficient number of *élite* from the masses ready to take their full share in the affairs of the community. For, by some irony hard to explain, it is generally the case that the more capable the so-called illiterate,

F

uncivilized masses prove themselves of gaining distinction in almost any field in any society offering opportunities for talent, irrespective of colour and creed, the more emphatic the assertion of racial dogma, the more inflexible and stringent the opposition to their emancipation.

6

The Paternal Posture

CHIKWENDA NWARIAKU

Nigeria

Chikwenda Nwariaku was born in Nigeria in 1929. He studied at
the University of Durham and at Imperial College, London. At
the time of writing his essay he was a post-graduate student in Civil
Engineering in Newcastle. He returned to Nigeria in May 1964.

I was born in Nigeria and have lived intermittently during the
past eleven years in most of the Western world, the greater part
of this external residence being in the United Kingdom. To that
extent, then, it may be fair to discuss this topic with the total of
these experiences, whether in the United States or France, or
Sweden, or other European countries, where colour discrimination has been 'observed'. My experience in my own country is
not helpful in this context because there is no colour discrimination in the negative, disruptive sense there. The Europeans who
live there are offered the best possible accommodation, they hold
the better appointments in the Civil Service as well as private
enterprise and they are not restricted as to their friendship or
societies. The agitation for Nigerianization is political in essence
and though directed at expatriates and therefore, as it were, at
people of a different colour, it lacks the primary motives and
feeling associated with colour discrimination such as national
arrogance, superiority or fear of economic insecurity. In fact, it
may be said that the agitation is a tendency to eliminate discrimination on the basis of colour. Unfortunately, other forms
exist among Nigerians themselves, the most disruptive being
discrimination on the basis of ethnic origin, popularly defined
as tribalism.

My background encouraged respectful contact with foreigners at an early age. Because my father was a civil servant I met several Englishmen. It is difficult to remember whether I had any special feelings of fear or curiosity. They lived in spacious bungalows in the reservations which they had selected themselves. We sometimes visited them and came away with gifts of mangoes and guavas and other fruits and vegetables. We often called at department stores managed by them and purchased tinned meats and other imported items like Ovaltine, Quaker Oats, white rice, sardines, tinned milk and some special or luxury items. There was no hostility and I remember that an Englishman kept our accounts and on some occasions actually offered us a lift to our house.

In secondary school, the exclusive school which the Methodists had established in an isolated clearing in the tropical forest at Uzuakoli, Englishmen, Scots and Irishmen had been our most respected teachers. These white men taught us the Christian religion, they opened to us the new vistas of the strange atomic theory, and inducted us into the philosophy of mathematics. 'Amazing race of people,' we thought. We admired them and played cricket and hockey with them, but we never for one moment thought that they either despised our race or suspected that their motives were anything but the purest and the best.

How and when does disillusion begin? In 1946, the senior students at our school organized a strike. In retrospect, I fail to understand the grievances. I was at the beginning of the third year of a seven-year course. Because of some mistaken assessment of my popularity with the younger students, I was inducted into the strike committee and instructed on what I should tell them about the proposed strike. I was expected to tell them about conditions ten years before, when none of that present generation of students was at the school at all. Perhaps because of excitement or out of loyalty to my seniors, I carried out my duties with my colleagues diligently. There was a strike and I was sent down. After an exchange of correspondence, my father took me up to school and it was agreed that I would be admitted on condition I submitted to six strokes of the cane. It was implied that that would be the only penalty. In an environment where birching was commonplace, six strokes seemed a ridiculous bargain and I readily submitted, worried more about making up lost time and regaining my position in the class at the forthcoming examinations. The decision was taken on a Friday afternoon and my father returned without me.

On Monday following, after morning prayers, it was announced that I should report to the Principal's office. I was not surprised and expected to collect my belongings which I hoped had been sent up during the week-end. The Principal himself was there to receive me and he was a man I respected, admired and perhaps feared. He epitomized authority and I believed that his word was gospel. He then ordered me to fetch a *machete* and further directed that, in company with two other colleagues, I was to cut the grass on the Old Field—one of the playing-fields of the school which was the size of a standard soccer field. The assignment occupied the better part of three days and at the end my palms were full of blisters.

I was certain I had heard his agreement with my father about the six strokes. Now my idol had failed. Disillusion had set in. I felt unable to trust not only my Principal, but also any other white man. Time has dulled the edges, but subconsciously the mark remains and, in moments of stress, it will not be surprising if it influences my attitude. But this cannot be interpreted as colour discrimination although somehow it was a feeling which I spread like a blanket over 'foreigners', and my education has done little to modify this critical experience. It is inconceivable that my Principal adopted this attitude because of my skin colour. On the other hand, with time and additional experience to call on, is it possible that he could not be complacent about a little Negro literally living on the edge of this primaeval forest and jungle, trying to undermine the authority of the ruling race and helping to create adverse publicity for his school which had a sound reputation for turning out first-class leaders. I may never know, but the disappointment has remained with me, although I do not believe that it consciously enters into decisions about my European friends and neighbours.

When does colour discrimination exist or is it a mental process real only to the mind of the victim? The paternal posture of the Geordie bus-conductor in Newcastle-upon-Tyne directing a confounded foreigner to a street or shop, the pat on the head or shoulder are in themselves quite natural and harmless. But when it happens to the graduate from Ghana or Uganda and not his colleague from Manchester or Carlisle, he wonders, perhaps mistakenly, if he is underrated. Was the conductor seeking confirmation that the black hair was really soft and woolly—an interesting topic of conversation with his wife at night—or was he treating this grown-up like a child because he was dark and therefore must be mentally young, or was the simple request for direction an opportunity to exhibit the divine right to guide the lower races? Or was the conductor, on the other hand, sincerely endeavouring to assist a welcome visitor in difficulty? Which is the true interpretation?

Is the shop assistant in a fashionable London store just in assuming that, because the customer may be an ignorant London Transport employee from St. Kitts or Barbados, she deserves no more than a brusque and grudging attention? Should the green-grocer, because you are black, decide which apples you may buy? On the other hand, she knows more about apples and may be faithfully trying to advise a foreigner who may be misled by colour.

The information services and the mass media have no difficulty in discovering that a man, who was burned to death in a tenement fire in Trafalgar Avenue, Whittle-le-Woods, Worcestershire, was Mr. John Bull Rutland, aged 34, that Rutland was married with three children aged 11, 5 and 6 months, that his wife was out shopping at the time. At other times, a nameless entity is run over or burnt to death in another blaze. This working, tax-paying entity, lying in a hospital morgue, known at the registry of births and deaths, is generally and invariably defined as 'a coloured man', incapable of having an address, never living in a town, having no friend, wife or children, and coming from anywhere between Pakistan and Jamaica. Is it that there is no space to give this information or is it that it is actually believed that Mr.

Rutland's death means something to someone somewhere, and that 'Coloured Man's' death cannot possibly mean anything to anyone, as 'Coloured Man' was never born and no heart-broken mother can exist anywhere for 'Coloured Man'?

Is it an accident that in the entertainment industry and, if one may be specific, the cinematograph presentation, the Negro invariably, until recently, denotes the whimpering, nauseating coward, fleeing before every real and imaginary danger, that he finds solace in the so-called spirituals instead of the ·22 Colt or Luger which his assailants understand better? It is not unusual that, in scene after scene, he only serves and waits on those who have a monopoly of affection, romance and love, those who exclusively feel joy and hatred, the love of children and indulgences of sex. The entertainment industry is specially important here because its power to create, manufacture and control public opinion and society is perhaps unequalled. However, on the colour question, it has assumed what may be described as a negative role, ostensibly because the public 'does not want it'. It is then to be assumed that the 'public', which can only imply a white public, wants the degraded Negro condemned to servitude while, at the same time, the public is agitating for independence and equality for this miserable section of humanity. No doubt it may be argued that some good reasons exist for the policy of the movie industry in the past, but such reasons have not occurred to me.

There are two more selective aspects of colour discrimination which I will now examine before passing on to other sections of this problem. The common incidents of discrimination are based on highly over-publicized cases in housing, membership of societies, availability of business credit and matters of that character. As in similar instances, they can be questioned and may in fact not be valid. The old lady who invites the Nigerian student to tea after an exciting lecture on the marriage customs of the Fulani people may not, in fact, have rooms to let when, after a week or two, the same student answers an advertisement for accommodation; it is for this reason that the so-called obvious cases are not given special treatment here and also because these are cases which, while adding to one's general attitude, are not so decisive as the less obvious examples.

What justification would the non-political, antidiscrimination student organizations such as the National Union of Students present for assuming that a 26-year-old science graduate from Uganda cannot be trusted to participate in a visit to Eastern Europe but are quite convinced that a 20-year-old fresher from Darlington is better adapted to resist Russian 'pressures'? Is it because the former, having obtained a first, is a soft intellectual 'egg-head' or is it that his membership of N.U.S. is of a different category which restricts the advantages of membership to visiting the ancient and lovely homes of England and the Pembrokeshire coast? One often comes against administrative reasons in matters of this nature; such administrative reasons may be justified the first and second time, but beyond that, it is difficult not to look for other reasons.

It is accepted here that a journalist who spent two weeks on the Moroccan coast is capable of discussing the whole complex situation in Africa from military uprising in Nigeria to the cost of living in Somalia. But it cannot be accepted either that a student who has spent six years in this country and has covered more ground than some of the native inhabitants is capable of discussing any aspect of the questions in this country, or alternatively that he knows enough about his own country to assist in informing the public objectively. Within the universities, it is not the foreign student who participates in 'international debates' or challenges assumptions about overseas education. Instead, by 'international' is meant a contingent from Edinburgh and Cardiff to Oxford. Finally, on this question of training and education, is it necessary that a Nigerian, trained in nursing in Nigeria by qualified sister tutors sent from this country, should be required to repeat three years of nursing training in Britain?

It seems perfectly normal that a Belgian Government can choose its own international friends and allies and enemies. The Americans are free to sell wheat to Russia, and students, civil servants, and scientists may be exchanged between both countries and, for that matter, this country, without general accusation of pro-Communism. If a Nigerian Minister had the courage to visit China, it would be a matter of hot speculation. There is the tacit assumption that no one, except the West, should be allowed to corrupt the sweet little African governments managed by Mr. Kenyatta and Tafawa Balewa and others. It is assumed that the Africans deserve to be ruled and guided indefinitely and that in this process, exclusive rights belong to the Western alliance and Free World. This aspect is brought in because it is an interpretation which grows on one during his residence in this country, and accounts for the difference in the reaction to international affairs between foreigners abroad and their citizens at home. The people in Ghana may not read in their papers that Britain is negotiating for orders with the Russians; they may also not read the speculation in this country about the projected visit of their Finance Minister to Prague, but the Ghanaian student here is at once exposed to both, and the native at home is spared the difficulty in reconciling this ambivalent situation.

Within this context is the indulgent, benign attitude, suitable for mentally retarded people and children, often shown to African leaders. They are cautioned against relations with governments whose leaders are entertained by the Government of this country. African governments may not exercise the rights and powers of governments to imprison or deport without immediate accusations of break-down in law and order. We have no right to a revolution because we are not experienced, and yet the oldest nations of the world, in Asia, have seen them, and this country weathered hundreds of years of this path to ultimate democracy and popular government. It is this particular aspect that concerns those who seek an international framework for solving the colour problem. It is also the most intractable, especially when each African Head of State who visits Britain cannot be accorded the simple courtesy of a Head of State; he is usually accused not of returning a courtesy call by the British Monarch but of seeking aid, loans, and advice. Such visits, instead of becoming opportunities for creating good-will, are exploited to ridicule customs and habits that are sometimes older than civilization.

The most difficult aspect of colour discrimination is encountered at the most unlikely intellectual levels and it is this aspect which is most agonizing. In 1959, at the beginning of the Central African crisis, a Peer of the Realm hurried back from Rhodesia to tell a packed House of Lords that a country of which he was once Prime Minister was populated entirely by liars— that all Africans are liars. This sweeping dogmatism is inexcusable among market women but a leader of public opinion had no hesitation in condemning a whole continent. It must be clear to anyone that it is untrue. It may be dismissed as an act of political irresponsibility from a frustrated politician. It cannot justify the slur. More recently, a Regius Professor of history glibly commented that there was no African history worth teaching, that it was only the history of Europeans in Africa. Is the history of Britain not as much a history of Romans in Cornwall, is European history not as much a history of Carthaginians and Moors roaming the Iberian Peninsula? It is not appropriate here to comment on this sad reflection on scholarship, and to sensitive minds, comments of that character are hard to explain except as expressions of racial and misguided arrogance which are justified only on grounds of colour. Since history is peculiarly a record of events, it is always there whether people are black or not; its progress is uninterrupted.

The expression of colour prejudice has been examined at length for two reasons. First, to indicate quite clearly that it is a classless phenomenon. It has been suggested by several apologists— that it is bred by ignorance and that it is peculiar to the lower classes of society and that when education broadens down to every man, the basis of colour discrimination will vanish. Secondly, the manifestations have been examined because of the assumption that they are limited to only a few 'obvious' sectors such as housing, recreation facilities and some other social amenities. In fact, these examples have been deliberately under-played because their ultimate contribution to the understanding of the colour problem in my view is secondary. For the same reason incidents in employment have not yet been mentioned. This category will be briefly discussed only to show the different variations of it.

On the one hand, immigrants may suffer through a deliberate policy of private enterprise not to employ non-natives. In the Civil Service, the standard required for civil engineers is different from the requirements for street cleaners or office porters but in both cases, some forms of discrimination may occur. In the one case, the engineering graduate, who is here deliberately to be trained and to return to useful employment in his country, is turned down because he 'cannot be expected to stay long enough with the organization', or the firm is 'interested in experienced people', and one wonders how the staff is renewed, especially when the advertisements in February and March specifically ask for young graduates. Moreover, the overseas student not unusually discovers that his classmates have been employed by the same firm which specializes in experienced staff. There are many reasons which justify these policies to those who adopt them but this cannot detract from the fact that those who, by this policy, deny the Sierra Leone Goverment the requisite member of trained graduate engineers, are the same groups who argue against building universities in Sierra Leone to train engineers, and argue against handing over power to Sierra Leone because they lack 'qualified men', who apparently are grown on trees and not in design offices and engineering works. At other times, the foreign student is 'too highly qualified for the requirements of the firm'. One is led to ask whether the organization is interested in morons.

The pattern for the unskilled is the same as for the skilled. The unskilled worker cannot understand the language and may not understand the public. But German and Swedish girls come to this country specifically to live and learn the language. Even this opportunity is not available and the Jamaican must already know the Queen's English in order to work on a building site with men who cannot write their own names.

The most emotive aspect of colour discrimination has been deliberately omitted from this examination. This is the question of so-called mixed marriages. I believe that this is a personal matter and, on the assumption that the British girl may or may not be capable of adjusting to the Westernized societies of Lagos, Kingston, or Accra, the decision must be taken by those who are directly concerned. It may be remarked, however, that the father or mother who loves Africans but would rather die than see their only daughter carried off to the 'jungle' to copulate and produce a litter of little dark bodies, needs to re-examine his attitude to international relations, world government and co-existence. It is perhaps within the sexual context that colour discrimination assumes its most ugly visage and the jealousy aroused by Anglo-Saxon girls deserting their real and potential boy friends for the 'virile' Negro bodies is at the root of some recent disturbances in some sections of this country. Those who hate and condemn this natural association between two human beings are blinded by their belief that the Negro is different and also inferior, and the sole basis for judgement is skin colour. This particular aspect is not limited to any class and its emotional root reduces the chances of rational cure.

Discrimination is indiscriminate in its incidence. It is based on colour. An angry bus conductor would as soon react against an Indian consultant as against a Nigerian freshman. The shop assistant would as soon despise the High Commissioner for Trinidad and Tobago as an able seaman from Accra. The only criterion is colour and this alone arouses resentment. Individuals are no longer individual. It is no longer a personal matter but a racial or continental crusade. You are not disliked or resented because it is you, Ahmed or Ihekwaba, but because you wear a particular type of skin. The casual remark of a police officer at point duty in the Strand may cause irreparable unspoken harm to Anglo-Congolese relationships because the Rolls-Royce Silver Cloud loses significance as a status symbol when the chauffeur-driven occupant, in spite of his pin-stripe and bowler hat, is dark.

The advantages of colour discrimination are dishonest advantages. The temptation to tell a police officer that you cannot understand English well in order to evade a traffic ticket, the awkward demands on indulgent landlords and others are alike deceptive and encourage the illusion and the myth that the Negro is different and must be treated differently and ought to be condemned. I can see no advantage in exploiting the colour problem for such mean gains and I see even less to justify any action which will encourage those who exploit it for wicked purposes, as examples in housing, crime, prostitution, and cheap labour indicate.

Whether the colour problem is susceptible to 'solution' is a question of how one interprets a solution. Regardless of parental attitudes, mixed marriages occur and will continue. Despite racial riots, young people of different races sustain healthy and fruitful associations, but the difficulty in accommodation and employment cannot be entirely eliminated even in the most homogeneous societies. There is no attempt to minimize the existence of this problem or to detract from the real suffering that it represents for many people, from the devotees of Oxfam to the more academic and habitual demonstrators for or against *apartheid* in education.

The primary task is not to solve specific problems which in the end are social problems but rather to examine those areas which create controllable discrimination. As an instance, it is possible to educate a child to accept a man as a man and still despise or hate him for his habits. To that extent then, the instruments of public opinion and information have a clear function. A simple experiment was carried out by the students' representative council of my university some time ago in connexion with accommodation. The landladies of the city were invited to tea and the question of housing was presented, not as a special favour of housing overseas students, but as a problem of housing people who were fit to be students of this university, people who were not only visitors from Lagos but also from Carlisle and Doncaster and Oxford, and, what was more important, the university desired the co-operation of the landladies to fulfil its purpose of providing not only mental but also physical comfort to those under its charge. The students were then accepted as students and many women, who had only thought of them as 'those people who should have remained in their country', were quite happy to shelter them and to enhance the brilliance of their stamp collections and Christmas cards with others from sunnier lands.

The attitudes that I hold on this matter have been developed since I left my own country. The process resulted directly from my presence here and opportunity for a broad education which it provided. In the political agitations which occurred in Nigeria in the early fifties, the colour question was hardly a matter that received any conscious attention and, in this respect, I have no built-in prejudices on the issue and, not having suffered any humiliation on these grounds, it may be assumed that I kept an open mind and to that extent this exercise is academic, as it may not be for Africans from some other parts of Africa.

Discrimination cannot be eliminated by legislation in most of the areas outlined in this essay, because most of the expressions are of the mind. The emergency of the War wiped out unemployment and only with full employment can job discrimination end. The same is true of housing and the expansion of social facilities and amenities. But in the inner recesses of the professor's mind, in the more shallow depth of the excitable Teddy-Boy's, the subconscious ideas and emotions that drive us to discrimination will remain. Circumstances may cause modification in outlook, but these cannot alter the differences that incite colour prejudice—colour itself. This will remain.

7

Racialism at the Meeting Point

FRANCIS M. DENG

Sudan

Francis Deng writes: 'I was born in 1938 in Abyei, administrative centre of the Ngok Dinka of which my father is the Chief. I had my school education partly in the South and partly in the North, racially distinct divisions of the Sudan. I studied Law in the University of Khartoum where I took part in organizing a programme of exchange of study-tours with European universities. This, with later individual initiative, made me travel extensively in Europe. After graduation, I was appointed "tutor" in the same university, and was later sent to London for my present post-graduate course (LL.M.) at King's College, London.'

IN our highly complex world 'progress' involves intricate paradoxes; gains and losses sometimes appear to cancel out. We are exhorted to draw much nearer in brotherhood than our grandfathers were. Nations do indeed now respond within hours to calls for assistance in any human disaster, whatever the colour, creed, or ideology of those in need. But side by side with this humane attitude is the gravity of the racial problem.

Modern communications have rendered tourism and immigration a lot easier than they have ever been. This fact, coupled with diplomatic courtesies and strategies, has encouraged a sudden coming together of people whose respective systems of education have not prepared them for an harmonious meeting; on the contrary, they have sometimes deeply rooted in them a strong feeling of contempt for each other. After the preliminary, superficial, attractions of curiosity—in themselves evidence of racial consciousness—the frictions appear.

Politically and socially, the *status quo* has changed rapidly. The ruled have become rulers. This change has meant equality between nations in international organizations; but even more notable, nationals of these newly independent countries have now the task of asserting their individual equality with others. In doing so, they are obviously questioning old assumptions that 'race' itself is a factor in making some superior to others. This is the origin of the wind of nationalism sweeping Africa today.

Such are the inconsistencies of our accomplishments; becoming more united in one humanity, acknowledging the integrity and competence of others by granting them the right to manage their own affairs, inviting people under our own roof as an expression of goodwill and assistance, at the same time we intensify mutual hatred by transforming what was latent prejudice and grudge into active indignation.

I speak of 'we' because in our heterogeneous world today it is difficult to conceive of a country where one will not encounter racialism in one form or another, although certain fields may be more explosive than others. Even as a child in the Sudan, I saw the reactions of one tribe to another, of one ethnic group to others, and of course, the attitude of foreign races towards our own. I am not assuming that I could define 'racialism' or even 'race' precisely, nor do I intend to do so; but in a broad sense I regard all these attitudes as aspects of racial consciousness. Some tribes looked down on others and would not inter-marry. It was normal for some groups to refer to others as 'slaves' because their ancestors had at times raided them in search of slaves. In fact, turning the clock back by twelve years, I recall one of my own experiences. I was walking along a sandy and lonely street one day with several members of my family. It was in a market town of the Baggara Arabs in the Western Sudan. As we walked, we came across a child of about six, playing with muddy sand so that he and his garment matched his surroundings. He got up, and gazing up at us steadily with an innocent smile on his face, he said, '*abiid*'. Taking it for '*tayibiin*' which is a greeting in that part of the world, we responded accordingly; but to our surprise, one of the party who had heard him rightly went up and slapped his face. We had little sympathy for the child when we knew that he had said 'slaves', though we could not help being amused. He was surely too young to know what he was saying, but he was clearly expressing the spirit of the community in which he was growing up.

I can quote, too, another case which illustrates the sense of racialism in the same setting. A prominent chief of a friendly neighbouring tribe wanted to marry into our family for diplomatic reasons. When the matter was put to the girl concerned, she objected to the suggestion. The Arab chief, in order to add weight to his proposal, sought the support of the British Administrator at that time, who tried to discuss the matter with our family and the girl. Writing about the incident, this Administrator reports: 'When I asked her about it, she laughed. "The man is all right," she said, "but he is an Arab. I'm a Dinka. We don't marry outside our people." '

Unfortunately, most Africans do not pay much attention to such cases, even though they may deplore them. Racialism to most people is a struggle between the Blacks and the Whites, usually taking the form of a colour-bar, or being given more definite form as a policy of subjection and segregation of the Blacks by the Whites. But history teaches that racialism is not necessarily 'colourism' and that it can be practised by Whites against other Whites. I have shown that race prejudice can be practised by Blacks against Blacks, though unacknowledged.

I must emphasize, however, that the black peoples are not unjustified in concentrating their detestation on racialism as practised by the white man against the black man. In the first place, the material superiority of the white man has made it possible for him to assert his might over the other groups. This naturally put all on equal footing of opposition against a common and greater enemy. As the power was monopolized by the white man no one else had the opportunity to display such disregard of others. In the second place, until the advent of European administration in Africa, most of these communities were separate and independent of each other, and however inferior each one thought the other, there was no question of really mastering one

G

another. Such sufferings as were inflicted on others through raids
and the like were like 'international' disputes—sometimes
governed by traditional conventions of reciprocity. In such
homogeneous societies as the African tribes, racial consciousness
existed, but was not emphasized. The foreign ruler came and
united peoples with little regard to their traditional ethnic
groupings; and as long as he remained, saw to it that no frictions
occurred in consequence. Racial antagonism is relative to the
interests in conflict; thus in Africa, whereas the educated *élite* and
the farmers deprived of land by settlers might join their efforts
against white domination, some isolated tribes tended to fear
neighbouring tribes with whom their interests conflicted, and
wish perhaps that white control could continue to safeguard their
immediate interests.

We were glad that our country was never really exposed to the
narrow meaning of racialism, i.e. as Whites versus Blacks. The
Europeans who went there were civil servants who enjoyed
privileges as such but never made it a permanent home. There
was no policy segregating the Blacks in favour of the Whites in
the manner we heard about to the east and south of our country.
We spoke, however, of the evils of racialism and objected to it
strongly, because it was practised against other human beings.
Worse still, to our mind, the victims were people whose fault was
to have the same colour of skin as ourselves—they were our
brothers in colour and in race. The less obvious problems of
racialism, such as the process of 'europeanizing' Africa, to which
we were also subjected, never occurred to us.

Such was my state of mind before I started travelling abroad.
Visits to England and Scandinavia, and also the mainland of
Europe, have sometimes magnified and sometimes modified my
feelings and thoughts about racialism.

In England, the problem of accommodation gives the 'coloured'
person the strongest, if not the only evidence of manifest racialism.
Whether it takes the form of the courteous and polite words
'sorry, just taken', when the stranger appears in person after a
telephone call, or the more blunt expression of 'regret, no
coloured', or the limitation to 'Europeans only', this experience

which is nearly always the first is likely to remain the worst. This is particularly true of those who have never personally experienced racial discrimination in their own backgrounds, whatever 'colour-bar' they may have heard of abroad. Such people have grown up thinking of themselves as people and not in relation to a superior race. Now—for the first time—they find themselves defined negatively as non-European, and discriminated against on that basis only. Again, they come in touch, for the first time, with the practical significance of the term *coloured* with *white* as the standard, instead of being called the black or the brown men they really are. Hardly anyone realizes the evaluations implicit in such terms. Yet in their innocent usage lies guilt. It reminds me of a telephone conversation I once had with a landlady in London. I was looking for accommodation. She asked about my nationality, and even when she knew I was Sudanese she couldn't quite make up her mind as to what colour she was dealing with; so she asked the relevant question 'Are you coloured?', to which I replied, 'No, I am black.' She was apparently sorry that our terms of reference were so different, and in her attempt to clear herself, she preached human brotherhood, explaining to me that she wanted to know whether I was white so as to inform me that she was accommodating Indians and Africans, and to ask whether I would put up with them. Whatever her real circumstances, I was surprised that she thought she could conciliate me by the reasons she gave.

The African is not a super-tolerant person, he is a normal human being, and perhaps more sensitive because of the situation in which a social revolution has placed him. Very few people would overlook these first impressions in search of the essential spirit of a society, and ponder the reasons behind such blunt expressions of racial prejudice.

What baffles me is that it is hardly possible to know whose attitude this discrimination really represents. One sometimes wonders where the responsibility lies. Those directly involved are often apologetic in their tone, implying that they acknowledge its unreasonableness. In practising discrimination, guilt shows itself on their faces. In some cases it may even be denounced by those who uphold it. At the bottom of the hierarchy of orders, particularly in accommodation bureaux, action is usually taken by innocent people who then have to face the bitter reactions of those discriminated against, and may perhaps be affronted by them.

It is hardly possible to come across anyone who has had to search for accommodation without experiencing racialism in one form or another. It would, however, be too short-sighted to conceive of racialism as only existing in such obvious cases of discrimination. These standard manifestations are indeed so clear-cut that they hardly need demonstration, but even what may not be discrimination at the outset may have racial consciousness implicit in it. Ironically enough, I found myself interested in observing the various features of racialism in Scandinavian and continental countries where one often meets the opposite of discrimination. Everywhere I went, in streets or restaurants, people approached me with friendly and sympathetic but very curious gestures. Some daring ones would suddenly spring on me to embrace me in friendship. At least a couple of times I had very embarrassing experiences in bars—people almost fought as to who should invite me for a drink. In another case a man who had just met me for the first time in a street, offered me money, and persisted so much that he gave way only after he noticed I was disturbed by the whole episode. I thought I was well-dressed and carried a brief-case and camera too, so that in my judgement no signs of obvious need were apparent.

Only too often in Sweden people would superficially praise the Africans to me and deprecate the Swedes for no other reason than that they were 'riding high horses', and too formal and exact about everything. I would listen without expressing an opinion as I became immune to such sweeping and irrational outbursts against Sweden by the Swedes. Every society has forms and conventions of its own which may differ from those of others, but bind people to a certain normative way of behaviour in that society. To conceive of Africa as a free domain without social norms is to construct a romantic dream-world.

I was often assured in a ludicrous manner that I was welcome to Sweden because 'we have no colour problems'. People would ask me about my feelings towards those obnoxious Whites who discriminated against the Blacks.

All this exaggerated and romantic kindness to Africans as Africans and not simply as persons has no roots and is not real. It at least indicates an unconscious racial consciousness, however sincere the immediate intention. It can even bring about a reaction contrary to what is expected. Indeed I rather ungratefully asked one man, who had welcomed me in the manner stated above, why he thought it necessary to advertise Swedish guiltlessness as if I had indicated any suspicions about it, for only those suspected of unreasonableness need prove the contrary. I have sometimes even found myself condoning the prejudices of the Whites simply to contradict an odd attack on the Whites by the Whites.

Such is the broader scope of racialism. It is too short-sighted to think of it only as discrimination. Both are branches of racial consciousness which the British and the French represented in their respective policies of segregation and assimilation in Africa. The roots of all are bound together. We may labour unnecessarily in demonstrating sympathy and maybe 'love' for others because we wish to rebut the presumption of hate or antipathy which is intrinsic in our character; we assimilate deliberately because we do not believe in the dignity of the other as a separate identity; and likewise we segregate because we do not honour the integrity of the other, and therefore prefer not to have ourselves polluted.

Most of these exaggeratedly friendly people, whether they are aware of it or not, believe that the African is a destitute who will rejoice to see a white man friendly to him, however impolite the manner of contact. Their approaches are therefore often very impudent despite their good intentions. They also believe that the Africans feel bitter against the white man as a race, and they deem it necessary to prove their innocence as individuals by attacking their group. Though a benevolent thought, this is likely to have an unfortunate effect on the African if not well-timed. It reminds him of the problem between him and his companion—that they are different and represent antagonistic racial classes.

This takes us to the even more occult but fundamental form of racialism which has been taking place in the process of 'europeanizing' Africa. It was implicit in the process of 'religionizing' and 'civilizing' the natives. African nationalism is now sweeping the Continent as a political movement, but it is in essence a racial impulse—the natural reaction by the negroid races against what has been a long indignity to their human qualities.

Under the colonial system the education of the African was generally styled in such a way as to uproot him from the soil of his origin and to isolate him from his cultural background. He immediately took pride in his newly acquired wisdom, and the change found roots in him. That is the tragedy. We have been made to believe in the inferiority of whatever is African. We grow up unaware of the riches which we possess in our music and dances, to give an example, and cut off from the social life of our people so that we are strangers in our own environments, and no longer understand the very people we are supposed to enlighten by the acquired rays of civilization. At Kirima, in Sweden, I once asked a Swede to put me in touch with an educated Lapp, and after giving me the address of an official in town he said: 'I don't think he knows anything about the traditions of his people. He is a civilized man.' That is the pride we win in Africa by being ignorant of our own selves. We only get to realize the need for knowing our values when it is almost too late, so that the inspiration only takes a romantic form sometimes detached from the reality. In fact, the vacuum for African values is better felt in Europe when the African realizes for the first time that he has always been just a copy of the European, with nothing primordial in him. He lacks the essential element of pride in having original values and an identity.

The general outcome of Western education is also projected on our political ideas and institutions. So conditioned are we in Africa that we do not want to build on them. Paradoxically enough we surpass the European in our irreverence for them. There are very few educated Africans today who do not attach a derogatory significance to the concept of 'tribalism', which is conceived of as reactionary, autocratic, and repugnant to nationhood. The general inclination is, therefore, towards its abolition.

In the field of conversion in Africa, the light of Christianity was not reflected in the traditional religious values. The explanation for this attitude is exemplified in the words of Sir Samuel Baker, the nineteenth-century traveller who wrote of the Nilotic people of the Sudan that they had no notion of God, 'nor is the darkness of their minds enlightened by even a ray of superstition'. Of course, this opinion is no longer considered valid, for since his time, many hundreds of pages have been devoted to the careful study of Nilotic religious practices and concepts, which have been shown to have much to teach us about the nature of religion. No religion grows in a vacuum. New religions may spring up or be imported merely to amend rather than replace those already existing. To import a religion *in toto* is to assume a spiritual vacuum in the context of the recipients, and to make such assumptions about human beings is to be contradictory in terms. Yet that is what happened in Africa. The indigenous religious practices were frowned on even if they were not judged repugnant to basic Christian principles, and of course, if they were so judged, then they were ferociously condemned. When transformation involves such deeply rooted ideas, there is bound to be a split in the personality of the convert, however much he may accept Christianity and all that it embraces. Moreover, the convert is regarded as a spiritual outcast by his own people; he is poised between two standards with divided loyalties to a divided conscience, and is denied the dignity of maintaining his original self. The integrity in the human experience of his race has not been acknowledged; and as mentioned elsewhere, the unavoidable reaction occurs when he realizes that he is just a faint copy, suspended between two worlds with nowhere to stand, because the manifestations of a people's religion and their culture are not severable.

Not entirely without justification, these realizations in the transformation of the African can bring about a blind emotional reaction that is unlikely to be fair to the Western world; and indeed how can one be fair if one has no criteria to apply, if one is deprived of one's self and one's pride in having personal values? That is the fate of the African. He has to alter course and catch up in the right direction; but in order to do this, he must totally surrender himself to a transformation. It is not at all the process that is painful, rather it is the knowledge that you are not what you were, the realization that you are not what you think you are, and the even more bitter and humiliating realization that you cannot be what you were. The more assimilated into new contexts an African becomes, the more vivid and honourable his original context appears to him. It is then that his present self and his lost identity combine to accentuate the pain he feels for being the African he no longer is, and the European he can never be, for the simple reason that he is not European. He has grown flexible adapting himself so much that he assumes a great deal of harmony which does not exist in reality. It is the revelation of this that causes his disillusion. No wonder, therefore, that the greatest advocates of the 'African personality' were tortured souls. If it were a matter of building a bridge between different attitudes it would pain less because one knows that the builders of a bridge must in any case cross with difficulty because they have no bridge to use.

All these changes were prompted by a firm belief that there could not be anything to build upon in such a 'primitive' world as Africa has always been depicted. They are the result of the general view that certain races are inferior with all that they have of ideas and practices; in other words, the natural consequences of racial prejudice.

Even now, where Africans are masters of their own affairs, the effects of their racial treatment show in their policies. African nationalism, as a racial reaction, can work in extremely different directions. Those whose reaction against African subjugation shows itself in the desire to be industrially equal with the West want a hurried transfer of Western achievements into Africa, so there is neither time nor inclination to investigate the impacts of Western civilization in general, particularly on those alien to it. These people conceive of emancipation as being similar to the

West, not merely equal with it. On the other hand, nationalism may take the very reactionary form of merely consolidating feeble African cultures weakened by the impact of what has been arrogantly assumed as superior culture. These people in their obsession tend to work for the revival and the maintenance of whatever is African to the exclusion of all other foreign ideas however useful, not because they regard these values as worth maintaining, but merely because they are African.

Most Europeans, on the other hand, may either desire and assist a radical change in Africa by the immediate importation of European industrial achievements, because they genuinely believe that Africa cannot have any virtues which might require proper study, and perhaps protection, in the process of industrial revolution, and they are so conditioned that they cannot see any alternative possibilities; or, they may discourage any change in Africa because of a romantic idea of retaining some variety in the world, to avoid the boredom of uniformity and similarity that might result otherwise. So, traditional Africa is to be protected in this sense, not because of its different virtues, but because it is something different, a kind of a resort from the pressures of civilization.

I should like to emphasize what I have already indicated elsewhere—we are all guilty of racial consciousness, both as classes and as races. It may be that the lower classes of the privileged races manifest their prejudice more than the others. This is because in relation to the 'inferior' peoples they feel dignity in being members of a 'superior' group and to change the *status quo* would be to create a situation of immediate competition between them and the promoted 'inferior'. Even if Blacks may be in fact more privileged in many respects, such 'inferior' white classes find gratification in their membership of a 'superior' race. In Europe it is these classes which feel the immediate impact of foreign infiltration. This does not, however, mean that they are the only racially minded groups. It is associated with the kind of interests in conflict. If we take, for instance, a more general field like racial antipathy in sex relations, we find an obvious involvement of all races and classes. Because of the strong emotions inherent in sexual matters, it wouldn't be an exaggeration to say that racialism is deepest rooted here. However broadminded we may profess to be, there is always a tendency, among all races and classes, to be very scrupulous about mixed marriages.

I shall not attempt to deal with the complex problem of the causes of racial prejudice, but to consider a popular view, it is generally believed that a race is inferior because of the inferiority of its material conditions. Its members are discriminated against because their conditions appear on them and repel more 'refined' people. There is naturally a strong element of psychological reaction against the unhygienic conditions of a race in materially inferior circumstances, but whatever the strength of this argument, it is only valid in so far as the defilement of the initial primitive conditions has been mystically cast on the race. It is no longer a matter of being personally abominable but of being a representative of that race. Of course, people discriminate for hygienic reasons even in their own racial groups. Once racial prejudice has been established by the material inferiority of a race, racialism develops more branches. The discriminating may indeed believe in the essential inferiority of the races discriminated against, and should the latter attempt to assert their natural dignity and equality, jealousy and fear may result.

It is also observable that where races differ, each race takes itself as the standard with all the others as abnormal cases. In this attitude is also implicit racial consciousness although only the one with the stronger hand can impose his superiority. My people have a saying that 'a gentleman of a tribe is unknown to a gentleman of another tribe'. Even if it is not necessarily a question of superiority or inferiority, there is often a failure to appreciate the other as a normal human being. I recall how amused we would be as children to see a white man eat *thau* fruits as a Dinka would. A *shilluk* friend of mine told me how he had often heard his people astonished to see a white man laugh 'like "the people"'. Note that the names of most Nilotic tribes in their traditional languages, literally translated, mean 'the people' with the rest referred to generally as 'the others'. Only in 1947 an official report on the Sudan included among other things this description of the people: 'Some of the natives are pigmies who catch game with poisoned darts. Some are cannibals with scarred faces—a different scar pattern for each clan. Others are giants almost seven feet tall who, like the Nile cranes, stand on one foot in the river for hours, looking for fish.'

As a result of our differences and mutual ignorance of each other, racialism occurs as a reaction at the meeting-point of races. The Dinka proverb says, 'In a strange home, the dogs bark.'

It all depends on what goal we seek; whether we aim at a fused world or would rather maintain the variety in races. It is not an easy decision to make consciously. It is often argued that the uniformity resulting from an amalgamation would be intolerably boring. On the other hand, one wonders how the course of events can be avoided. Facts show that this mixing of races has already commenced and modern conditions are facilitating it. Such a coming-together is necessary if there is mutual need for each other, which there appears to be. It may be that our fears of boredom are only conditioned by the present state of affairs, and as our sentiments are likely to alter with the change of circumstances, we cannot quite predict how we shall feel in an amalgamated world. What is most important in this respect is that such fusion of races should be in an atmosphere of goodwill and mutual respect, so that we can derive the maximum benefit from the variety in our values as races. To adjust ourselves to the values of one race will be to abandon indiscriminately a long chain of human experience with all the values of the others, most of which we have not even attempted to know. That would be a loss to the entire humanity—a remote but an everyday tragedy.

Be all that as it may, in view of the inevitability if not the desirability of coming together, the sooner the reaction takes place the better, for only after realizing that the others are after all not as different as we had conceived, and even more fundamentally that they share in our humanity, can harmony be hoped for. What makes each one of us a 'moving circus' in a different racial context except for the fact that we fail to take each other as normal human beings? It was because of such public curiosity that my German hostess, in a very remote part of the Black Forest, once remarked, 'I am sure we would gain a lot of money if we put you in a circus.' The reaction could not take the form of contempt for each other if we realized the dignity each race puts on its own self—the universal dignity of the human race. How many Europeans hear of Africa and imagine a world where man and beast are inseparable?

Equipment for such a harmonious meeting can only be hoped for from education in the very broad sense of the word. All conceivable ways and means should be mobilized. But the trouble with such a process is that it is itself conditioned by the very problem it tends to solve so that progress is often very slow. The Press and other means of mass-media could facilitate such education. As the situation is today, however, commercial interests unfortunately need sensation and truth is usually too cold. Only too often when a white man disappears in the impassable jungles of Africa, European reporters suspect cannibalism, and the facts now and again prove them wrong. What human purpose can possibly be served by such vulgar jokes as I once saw in a Swedish newspaper which caricatured two African girls talking: one said: 'I saw you yesterday with a missionary, who was it?' 'That was my lunch,' replied the other. Funny, but obviously detrimental; for when they concern the dark continent of Africa who can tell jokes from facts?

Another way of aiding understanding would be to encourage exchanges in the form of study-tours between school children and university students during their vacations, to bring about a mutual appreciation of each other's values, thereby fostering mutual respect. To meet a man under his own roof is to realize his independent integrity whatever material conditions he may be in. That is why one-way traffic can be quite harmful. Besides, at least at these early stages, the quality and perhaps the numbers of people at these meeting-points should be controlled to some extent, because indiscriminate meetings can do more harm than good. Obviously, we all have something to be proud of and something to be ashamed of, and it wouldn't be an unwise 'face-saving' device to limit the exportation of what may discredit us, and perhaps cause a certain delay in the achievement of our more fundamental human fulfilment.

In addition to these long-term designs, other immediate means could be applied. It may be necessary to use the law where reasonable in the circumstances without unduly fettering individual freedom. Moral law and secular law are quite complementary and although it is usually the public conscience that makes the law, law in its turn may procure public conscience. This should, however, be approached most carefully, because to eradicate racial prejudices we need to establish love for humanity as represented by all races, and love is a self-revealing inner quality which can never be dictated by law.

The time has arrived when good faith must be manifested. The world is tending more and more towards one domestic unit, and should any race suffer from human vices, it is likely to infect us all. The immediate responsibility lies with those whose power has enabled them to impose their racial superiority. On them rests the moral obligation to undo what they have done. The reaction of the depressed races is reaching a dangerous point. I met an American journalist whose spirit very well illustrated what this reaction can mean; 'I am not a Black Muslim', he declared, 'but I believe that the white man is inferior, and that is why it takes him such a long time to convince himself that he is not. He does not understand the language of love represented by such people as Martin Luther King. The only language he understands is "If you step on my head, I will step on your head." They are through! Believe me! They are through!'

When racial prejudice ceases to be a natural and spontaneous reaction and is transformed into blind policies to serve the nepotism of truculent people, the theory of right and wrong comes to an end and justice can only achieve itself when the ill-treated break the chains of subjection and free themselves by the iron arm. Lord knows what next. This now seems the inevitable and disastrous conclusion to the determined struggle against racialist masters by subject peoples. Nationalism is a reaction to injustices imposed upon a person who thinks better of himself than he is depicted. It is an assertion of one's rightful place in the values of human dignity and integrity. The African will find it too hard to fight twice against hate—hate in the white man and the even stronger hate now growing in the fertile soils within his heart well manured by white policies. This applies equally to any kind of racialist domination. 'He strikes hardest who strikes last.' I speak of Africa as a whole, for what a man suffers in any part because of his colour touches the heart of the man in another area and causes him to panic. So long as they share the same 'disadvantage' of colour and 'race' they are two in one.

Will human history continue to be one of hatred *ad infinitum*? Even when it is not a policy racialism is a serious moral challenge —a problem which should no longer be treated as a series of isolated facts, but as a universal and deeply rooted vice of which we are all guilty, whoever and wherever we may be. Our moral weakness lies in our reluctance to judge ourselves by the same criteria by which we judge others. We all need to educate ourselves, to relax at the meeting-point and accept our differences as facts which are overwhelmed by the unifying factors of a common humanity. Let us then start by acknowledging ourselves as patients who all need treatment whether racialism is active or latent in us. Racial consciousness is the root of racialism, discrimination is only a shoot; destroy the roots and the shoots will wither away.

8

The File of Regrets

SYED ALI BAQUER

India

Syed Ali Baquer was born in 1937 in India and studied sociology
for his B.A. and M.A. degrees at Osmania University, Hydera-
bad. He worked as a Welfare Officer in the field of rehabilitation
of released prisoners before coming to England to attend the
United Nations Congress on Crime Prevention which was held
in London in August 1960. He stayed in England and is at present
doing a course in Social and Administrative Studies at Oxford
University.

MY attitude to the colour problem before leaving India was 'I
don't mind the Coloureds.'

My knowledge of the problem came from my university
training in sociology both at graduate and post-graduate level
and from the personal accounts of my family and friends who had
lived abroad. A cousin of mine returning from Little Rock in the
late fifties gave me a personal account of the 'unfortunate disturbances' there. Another close friend described the 'savage
instances' of Notting Hill and Nottingham and spoke of the
increasing intolerance of the British public towards the coloured
people. The above two and many other informants who described racial riots showed real concern towards the growing
tension but without betraying the slightest degree of involvement.

A brief account of my familial, educational, and social background will serve as an index of my general outlook and expectations.

Since the turn of the century innumerable members of my
large family have studied in Germany, Great Britain, and

America. They returned to exalted positions and enjoyed improved prospects, prestige and standards of living, and became the social *élite*. For decades there has been a constant flow of young men and women returning from Europe after spending the most formative years of their lives there. The advantages of spending a few years abroad were too obvious to the 'pundits' of my family to be discussed. The progressive outlook and keen sense of duty of these 'foreign returned' people gave an over-glamourized picture of Western education to the rest of the family. Its value was never questioned or challenged.

Conformity to the Western way of living was appreciated and encouraged. My family, on the whole, found a happy medium between the East and West. The atmosphere in which I was brought up sanctioned a certain amount of freedom to the young. Mixed swimming parties and moonlit night walks were not infrequent. Religion was mostly a matter of convenience and slight deviations from long established customs and traditions never brought much criticism.

There was nothing unusual or spectacular when I announced my intentions of leaving home for England. The aspirations of the ambitious young were always fixed on going abroad. The only person really concerned about my proposed departure was my father. He explained to me that due to increased expenditure and decreasing income it would be very difficult for him to support me financially during my stay abroad. The objections of my father to my adverse economic circumstances could have prevented me from leaving home but I was selected to attend the United Nations Congress on Crime Prevention as a delegate. Therefore the first fortnight in the United Kingdom had some purpose and my board and lodging were secured. Meanwhile I was able to get in touch with several friends who had been to the same schools and colleges at home. I was also able to contact an English film producer whom I and my family knew from his stay in India.

I had met a great many Americans, Europeans and Englishmen before coming to the United Kingdom. I was very well-informed of the general habits of British people. My knowledge of London was correct down to minute details. My first impressions of England were not different from those of a holiday-maker who had been carried away by the poetic descriptions of a travel agency brochure. But no matter how much literature one has read about the country he intends to visit, experience always teaches him some more.

To be labelled 'coloured' was not exactly painful in the early stages but instead appeared to be very interesting. I was gradually made aware of the full significance of racial prejudice. Disappointments and the frustrations that followed them damaged my optimism about the life in Great Britain to a considerable extent. I had to reconcile myself to the fact that I—an Indian with a 'golden sun-tan'—was also a coloured man in the eyes of English people and therefore subjected to certain popular discrimination. But my keen desire to have new experiences and to explore new ground lent me courage to struggle in the face of the disappointments that were to follow. My account is mainly the personal impression of a young man who was forced into the coloured camp because of his subordinate economic position and who stayed there voluntarily to face the music on his own. It is therefore very subjective and is not a piece of scientific research.

Bus crews were provided with hostel accommodation in Oxford, and this determined my first employment. I was given a brief and formal training with five or six others who started with me and no special attention was given to the fact that I was a foreigner and that my requirements were slightly different. Outside working hours I was left on my own to find ways to fill up the time. There were many other coloured conductors who were only too ready to volunteer information which could make any newly arrived person frightened. These are the people who not only influence but practically mould the attitude of the newcomer. They exaggerate their bitter experiences. Their tales have lost force with repetition but they expect all others in their position to share their views. I was once given a farthing as a sixpenny bit and did not realize my mistake until late that evening the cashier returned the coin to me. The comment of an

H

experienced coloured conductor was: 'You've got to watch 'em, sonny. These people always cheat you.' I was naturally very alert the following few days and examined every coin and suspected every single passenger. Weeks later after receiving several thousands of genuine coins I could get over that comment. That cheated coin could have been a mistake. My own rationalizations did not let me connect such and similar minor instances with the skin pigment as most of my 'friends in colour' were hasty to do. A little guidance from my employers about dealing with people and other occupational hazards could have made the race relations much more pleasant. But failing this, prejudice becomes the obvious conclusion. Prejudice breeds prejudice, and yet little or no work has been done on the attitude of the coloured workers towards their white counterparts.

I had worked as a welfare officer in the field of rehabilitation of released prisoners before coming to England and was therefore convinced that I deserved a better job and constantly tried to get one. If the qualifications of a young man who has taken his medical degree at an Indian university are acceptable and the lives of people could be entrusted to him, then, I was tempted to think, why should a graduate of the same university be offered menial jobs? The high wages were responsible for the apparent adjustment I had made to occupational downgrading. I was very sensitive to my new status, and even though I discharged my duties to the utmost satisfaction of my superiors, work-mates, and passengers I never could take pride in my appearance or work. There were other compatriots who wore their uniforms smartly and decorated their jackets with badges, etc. When in one of his letters my father insisted on knowing the exact nature of my job, I answered very cautiously that it was 'highly lucrative and involved dealings with the public and their money'.

The effects of my occupational status were two-fold. First, I felt that my position in Great Britain was that of an uninvited guest and therefore I had no right to make any claims and should not expect the British society to extend a more positive welcome and a nice cushy job. I could not grumble. Secondly, I was looking forward to full participation in all spheres of cultural and social life. The opportunities of any such social intercourse were denied to me, not so much because of the colour of my skin, but due to the fact that I belonged to the working class. (And I belonged to the working class because I was an unwanted and uninvited guest. It was a vicious circle.) I did not mind this restricted existence in the beginning but when the novelty of that new adventure was worn out, it became almost imperative that I should either get a white-collar job or else work in a capacity which was less exposed to the public eye than that of a bus conductor.

Finding a suitable job proved to be a very difficult task. It is generally believed that if employment is available in abundance, the colour of the skin does not remain important. After all the buses must run; dustbins must be emptied. The very assumption that the coloured people are best suited for dirty menial work irrespective of their qualifications causes much unpleasantness. But with regard to good jobs, the labour market in this country is governed by some unpredictable laws of supply and demand. For months I kept on applying to every single advertisement that I set my eyes on in the local newspaper. If I mentioned my nationality the Post Box Numbers hardly ever bothered to answer the application. And all others who did answer never had anything to offer to me. Their letters of rejection I have filed in the 'File of Regrets' in chronological order. Out of the dozens of applications I wrote, only three did actually short-list me for an interview and on one occasion, in fact the only occasion, I had the privilege of rejecting the offer of working as an Assistant Grounds-man in a local school. In response to one particular advertisement for the post of a clerk which appeared in the newspaper for months on end, I continued to apply at set intervals presenting my qualifications in as persuasive a way as possible. But the answer was the same. I did not have to read it.

I do admit that most of the workers who seek employment in this country are unskilled, uneducated and unqualified but I strongly object to the practice of employment exchanges of offering coloured men certain types of jobs. In any discussion on these problems I have found that people tend to confuse two separate issues and get hot under the collar instead of finding a solution. The question 'Who asked the coloured people to come to this country?' should be treated differently from 'What should be done about them since they are here?' There is not much sense in directing a physically feeble person to work on a building site just because he has a different complexion. True, employers find difficulty in communication with some of them because they cannot speak English, but there is a considerable number of immigrants who do not speak any other language but English and yet they find themselves getting the same treatment. The authorities, perhaps in an attempt to solve the employment situation as a whole, tend to treat the immigrants as a homogeneous group. No one wants to be deprived of his individuality and any such generalizations could lead to serious misunderstandings. After a few years study of the problems of coloured labour I have come to the conclusion that the attitudes of the British authorities in directing the coloured labour to existing vacancies are very discriminatory. It would indeed be more desirable to make a more sympathetic assessment of individual needs and then to allot suitable jobs according to respective potentialities. To meet the demand for a certain type of labour the authorities will go on turning to the imported supply that has no other value in the labour market. A change in the present attitude and practices of the Employment Exchange is most certainly needed. If tolerance were shown in this respect only then could it be fair to anticipate that the employers would stop insisting on the theory that 'beggars can't be choosers'. The immigrants should be able to get employment according to their merits and not their appearance.

My next job was as a porter at the local teaching hospital. I worked there for nearly twelve months in various departments and had the opportunity of studying the hierarchy of hospital administration. Porters were never treated as Whites or Blacks. They were just porters. Any attempt to cross the intangible frontiers was disapproved. People who are insensitive to their low status are definitely fortunate. Most of us willingly put up with the work, the coloured ones especially avoiding conflict by making fewer demands. A worker shows greater efficiency if the chances of his getting another job are remote. There are very well-defined grades of respectability in a teaching hospital and one does not find any difficulty in knowing his own position in the hierarchical order.

I had felt the snobbish indifference of my compatriots, who were studying at various colleges at Oxford, even when I was working as a bus conductor and ascribed that attitude to the general 'town and gown' feelings one experiences in Oxford. A hospital is a very small and compact society and people are bound to see each other over and over again. The effort with which the coloured doctors avoided the coloured porters was conspicuous. The well-placed immigrants adopt the social customs and practices of the society which has offered them a superior position to such a great extent that they look down upon their own compatriots. But paradoxically, one can detect a deep feeling of shame on their faces when they are confronted with a fellow-being who is engaged in some menial work. I used to think before leaving home that anyone would be pleased to see his countrymen thousands of miles away from his home. This attitude could not be interpreted as class consciousness because the very same people are very civil and polite to other white men doing the menial jobs. I found this colour antipathy shown by my own people the most pathetic of all prejudices. These people believe that social distance alone could maintain their social status and any association with the working immigrants would jeopardize their own position in the eyes of their friends. They suffer from a more acute class-cum-colour consciousness than the British.

As a porter I had tea at the Porters' Lodge but when I became a clerk I was not only allowed but was welcomed to have tea with the doctors and consultants. As soon as I took off my porter's uniform I became a normal human being in the eyes of the superior group. But the only people who did not accept me in my promoted role were, ironically enough, the coloured doctors.

The housing shortage in Oxford is difficult but it was bad enough in my own city in India. The British Council offers no help to non-students and its activities are restricted to students who have come to Britain on handsome scholarships or grants and are prepared to pay exorbitant rents. Another social organization, perhaps in a desperate attempt to help me, directed me to one particular house which was known to them for overcrowding. One more immigrant, they thought, would not add to the existing chaos. (Strangely enough it was the same organization which, months later, sought my help to assist the Public Health Officer in solving the overcrowding problem of the very same house.) With a printed list of lodgings which was given to me by a kind-hearted landlady I went on an unsuccessful and unpleasant pilgrimage of house hunting. My need was not urgent as I was staying in the hostel run by the bus company. I eventually did find digs in the house of a Pakistani labourer.

Even when I did not need accommodation for myself I made house-hunting my leisure-time hobby and used to apply in person, mostly dressed in uniform, to as many advertisements as was humanly possible. This unorganized survey of the attitudes of landladies proved to be highly entertaining. I was looking for explanations for the difficulties of finding accommodation and as a result acquired a deeper insight into the factors that force immigrants to live in condemned houses and filthy sanitary conditions. Instead of getting bitter I used to enjoy the embarrassed expressions of the landladies who did not want to have coloured immigrants as their lodgers. Some of them lacked the courage to confess their preference for white lodgers. On several occasions I had to insist that a particular landlady whose room was always taken 'the night before' should remove the notice from the shop window in front of her house.

Now I have come to the conclusion that prejudice is exercised against immigrants. It is, however, perhaps easier and more justifiable for a landlord to refuse to let his rooms to anyone he does not want to mix with than for an employer who is subject to public pressure. Besides, the employer does not have to live with a person he does not trust. The landlords and landladies have only a stereotype picture of the coloured immigrants and as it happens to be a particularly undesirable image of 'strange' people, they show reluctance in opening their houses to immigrants. If the coloured man happens to have a college scarf round his neck the landlady finds it easier to expect a certain standard of behaviour. As a student it was easier for me to get suitable accommodation. But once a comfortable room has been found, and a harmonious relationship established with the landlady and co-lodgers, there remains no ground for any unpleasantness on this account. I at least did not have to change my digs frequently.

Immigrants generally expect that the host community will accept them without any hesitation. Assimilation is a slow process. It becomes all the more difficult and complicated if the immigrants do not share the same norms and value judgements as the host community. Asians do not adapt readily to the British society as they have their own counter-weights of culture and religion. I adjusted to my physical and human environment without much strain but my subordinate economic position made me a victim of class stratification. As a foreigner I was handicapped by an inability to impress the people I talked to with my accent. It became necessary after some time to express very clearly that I was not just a part of the filthy bus but something more. Beating one's own drum is not easy but my attempts to 'break the ice' did not remain unrewarded for long. Invitations to social gatherings and also to visit families began arriving and I made some very interesting and useful friends. One contact led to another and within a few weeks my whole leisure time was taken up with such engagements. One family in particular took special delight in arranging talks on various Indian topics for some local social organizations like the Young Wives and Young Farmers. Some of the people who really never came into contact with the coloured people were pleasantly surprised to discover that all immigrants are not alike. I felt happy in acting as a self-appointed ambassador of the coloured population. I could make the British people see that lack of insight into individual differences could be seriously misleading.

It will be worth mentioning here that only three persons out of hundreds I worked happily with ever invited me to their homes.

The British people do not entertain their workmates at home and the immigrants do not generally appreciate this. It has very little to do with the colour of the skin. A Ukrainian family I stayed with for nearly one and a half years has been in this country for over fifteen years, and Englishmen were rarely present among their many visitors. But the tragedy of the immigrants, and more particularly of the Asians, is heightened by the fact that the only point of contact between them and the native population is the work situation, and if they fail to strike a relationship here, they never get invited to British houses. Students from abroad are better placed in this respect. I know a number of people who have never stepped inside a British house though they have been in this country for years. No wonder their way of living is basically unchanged.

Even though I respect the sincerity with which the visits to British families are organized and the way the coffee evenings are arranged for 'visitors from abroad' and 'the lonely foreigners', I found a majority of them formal, unimaginative and exhausting. One met the same or similar people, who out of some altruistic motive had undertaken to play a polite and social role. I am often surprised at the attempt of most immigrants to conform to the anticipations of the British people in simple things. How on earth can a person who has been roasted in scorching sun all his life grumble about the cool sky covered with beautiful grey clouds! How can anyone resent the charm of a misty morning or the romantic vagueness of a foggy evening! How can one help but appreciate the inviting whiteness of snow-bound earth!

In my social encounters with the British people I found some very well-informed about the social, economic, and political situation of my country. There were some who had served in India at one time or other and those 'sahibs' who had had good times there showed greater tolerance and understanding than others. But there were some whose ignorance about a country which was a 'jewel in the British Empire' was amazing. I do not feel hurt now if someone insists on representing my country as a land of snakes and crocodiles and rope-dancers. In one coffee-evening the innocent curiosity of an enthusiastic college-girl proved to be very entertaining when she turned to a Nigerian standing next to me and asked in an affected accent: 'And what did you exactly feel when you saw a white man for the first time?' 'Found him a bit appetising,' I could not resist interrupting. Such well-intended remarks hurt the immigrants and the irritation resulting from them makes the newcomers believe in the existence of colour prejudice.

An occasional visit to a family could prove very tiresome because of extreme formality, exaggerated hospitality, and deliberate patronizing. My experience has taught me that to know a few, or even one family is far more satisfying than acquaintance with a large number of people. In a foreign country it is not so much the strangeness of physical environment or the uncertain attitude of the people that depresses the immigrant, but it is the absence of primary relationships which makes his adjustment difficult. Perhaps it is because of this emotional need that an immigrant looks for satisfaction among the opposite sex. A satisfactory sexual or emotional life could minimize the frustrations of an immigrant to a great extent. At least he thinks so, and since as a foreigner he does not have an established social life, he spends most of his time in places where he is bound to see many young couples. It makes him all the more conscious of his loneliness and consequently he resents the fact that he is being treated as an untouchable. As a conductor it was a lot easier to talk to the girls than to the boys, but on the other hand, old ladies were more difficult to get on with than the old men. Continental girls on the whole were very easy to mix with. Their frustrations as *au pair* girls and hospital maids are not much different from the experiences of the immigrants save for the colour of the skin. They are attracted to coloured people either out of curiosity about the dark complexion or because of a deep desire to defy British views. As strangers to this country they find greater freedom than their British counterparts. But going out with white girls causes much rivalry and jealousy between the host community and the immigrants. The British girls who do go out with the coloured people are either not well-placed in their society or suffer from some physical handicap. Attentions paid by occasional homosexuals and nymphomaniacs are far from flattering and the process of endless search for a suitable companion adds to frustrations. As meeting with girls was not taboo in the society I come from I do not place undue emphasis on sex. Therefore my approach to them has always been straightforward and uninhibited. As a working-class man it really was very difficult for me to take girls out without creating some problems for them. One such girl who was seen with me became the centre of criticism. One of her well-wishers who was thinking of 'her own good' asked her in front of me: 'What do you think your parents would say if you go home with a coloured child?' The poor girl was too confused to answer so I had to ask: 'What do you think her parents would say if she goes home with a white child?' But my friends of both sexes have multiplied in geometric progression since I joined the university.

The operation of racial prejudice is said to be very open in dance-halls. I have been refused dances scores of times. It is a very common experience of coloured people that the girls who refuse to dance with them accept the invitation from the white boys. Such an attitude is readily interpreted by the coloured people as colour prejudice. Though not a good dancer myself, I like dancing and visited a particular dance-hall for weeks in order to study this problem. I discussed the issue with several girls from time to time and the total impression from the reasons offered by them shocked me by its very simplicity. The girls, like the rest of the population, had a stereotyped image of the young immigrants. These men, it was said, do not come to dance but to pick up girls. If a girl dances with one coloured man he feels that she has been attracted towards him and grossly misunderstands her motives. He then persuades her to stay with him all through the evening and she finds herself separated from her other friends. She has to listen to accounts of his home-sickness and of the colour prejudice he has experienced in England. He exaggerates his account so much that she cannot help but feel sorry for him. He exploits the situation further by asking her in most pleading language to come out with him. It is not always easy for her to handle the situation without either hurting him or getting herself involved in some future commitments. So to avoid all this she says 'no' to the first request. But with her own countryman she knows exactly where she stands. She dances with him and if there is no mutual liking that is the end of it. Since some of the coloured people are very good dancers, she does not find it unreasonable to enjoy dancing with them, but as it invariably becomes a source of bewilderment she prefers an Englishman as her partner. Another important point generally overlooked by most men and misunderstood by the coloured men is that when a boy requests one girl out of a row of girls and she says 'no' for one reason or another he immediately turns his attentions to the girl seated next to her. No girl wants to be the second choice, and therefore many reject the offer. Whatever the reasons, the display of colour discrimination in dance-halls is obvious. Its intensity could be debated and its operation rationalized. But rationalization and logical explanations cannot be substitutes for a dancing partner.

The attitude of 'cold and reserved' British people is completely different when they are faced with an Indian girl. My own cousin, who came to England after me and worked in a big departmental store as a shop assistant, always got very warm and friendly attention from all the people she came into contact with. The very same people who never 'break the ice' actually took steps in making her stay extremely pleasant. She went back after a few months, but to her Britain would always remain a country full of very warm-hearted people whose hospitality to her was overwhelming.

It is the demands an immigrant makes on a host community that make the hosts critical of his presence. A friend of mine who is a professional actor in India recently visited Great Britain and stayed here for a couple of weeks. He met the British families I have now known for years and my other friends at different colleges and also went to several parties. The performances of his mime art were very popular. He never mentioned colour prejudice during his entire stay. Those who expect nothing are the least disappointed.

As I wanted to base this essay on my personal experiences I

have tried to avoid drawing any conclusions distinctively based on my more general impressions of the colour problem. Mine has been a purely descriptive account. Any generalizations about my fellow immigrants and their behaviour in this country demand a more thorough study of historical evidence and of the social sciences. I have written this essay at a time when it was easy for me to look back. Time and subsequent pleasant experiences have healed many wounds. Details of many experiences have become dim and their significance has been lost. It is so easy to appear calm over certain things that once needed an extraordinary control of one's feelings!

9

Colour and Equality

S. WEERAPERUMA

Ceylon

S. Weeraperuma was born in Ceylon in 1934. He is a B.Sc. (Econ.), London, and Chartered Librarian (A.L.A.). At present he works as an Assistant at the National Central Library. At the same time he is reading for an M.Sc. in Economics and for the Bar Examinations at Lincoln's Inn. In the future he would like to continue working as a librarian or do university teaching. He describes himself as 'a bachelor, vegetarian, teetotaller, non-smoker, pacifist and agnostic'.

FEW investigations into the colour problem have been impartial, for often the inquirer has been biased. This bias was actually the result of certain hidden forces at work in the racial unconscious. Therefore the examination of oneself seems an obvious preliminary requirement for the investigation of the colour problem. Recorded below are the efforts of painful self-scrutiny.

As my entire boyhood was spent in Ceylon, where the vast majority have a brown complexion, the colour problem then interested me only theoretically. Therefore surprise rather than horror was the reaction to discriminatory incidents in Europe and elsewhere which were reported, often in a magnified form, in Asian newspapers.

It was the prevalent tendency in intellectual circles to suspect the good faith of all European countries which interfered in Asian politics. All Europeans were generally regarded as the representatives of the exploiting and oppressive colonial countries. In such a context the Indian struggle for independence passionately interested me, but not primarily as a colour problem. I had been influenced by the teachings of Mahatma Gandhi to the effect that the Indians had nothing against the English as persons but were united in their opposition to the evil in foreign rule. India was torn by racialism, religious bigotry and the snobbery of the caste system but there, just as in Ceylon, no recognizable colour problem existed. This was because the populations in this part of the world comprised persons of almost every shade of colour.

That human beings had varying complexions was a fact I had no difficulty in accepting. The trees, leaves, flowers, animals and other objects that arrested my attention as a child lacked a uniform shape and colour. Colour and variety in the universe not only intensified the sense of wonder but added to the joy of living. It is noteworthy that often the upholders of segregation believe in a uniform world. Circumstances in childhood help to mould the view that the world consists or should consist only of Whites, and when this illusion is challenged by actuality the sense of smug security gets disturbed.

Children are indifferent to the perverted distinctions that are drawn by supposedly more mature adults. The child in its innocence does not discriminate on the ground either of the social status or of the colour of its playmates. In India the Brahmin child mixes freely with the so-called low caste child. It is one of the sad facts of existence that in the process of attaining physical maturity most people seem to destroy what is innately human in themselves. As this degradation is almost universal it points to unsatisfactory education. Recalling my childhood, I should observe that certain Buddhist priests in Ceylon tried to inculcate an antagonistic attitude to all non-Buddhists in the country, particularly the Tamilian Hindus and the Ceylonese Christians. Fortunately I escaped this early brainwashing. I felt it intrinsically cruel to create divisions among men who belonged to one species. My sentiments have been epitomized in the words of Robert Frost:

> Something there is that doesn't love a wall,
> That wants it down.

It cannot be honestly stated that my playmates were so innocent as to let differences in complexions pass unnoticed. Certain boys were considered more handsome because their complexions were lighter. A certain unattractive Eurasian boy was considered handsome merely because he was fair. The underlying factor here seemed to be the preference for an ugly but fair person to a handsome but dark person. The reason for this unfortunate distortion of aesthetic values was the unconscious admiration for the then ruling European races in Asia. Though consciously I disliked the alien rulers, unconsciously there was a raving admiration of the power and might of the white races. I secretly wished to become identified with the dominating countries and 'europeanize' my pigmentation if possible!

A part of my education was in a Christian school. The manner of several European Christian teachers was superior and priggish. When it came to imparting religion, the personality of Jesus was presented as an awe-inspiring civilizing force from the European world. Christian art, murals and Christmas cards conditioned the formation of a mental image of Jesus. In a childlike way I imagined a tall, fair, and bearded man with flowing blond hair. Perhaps Christian children throughout the world picture this apostle o universal love likewise. If Jesus were depicted with a slightly tanned Middle-Eastern complexion (as was probably the case) it might result in a more sympathetic attitude towards coloured people throughout the Christian world.

It is, incidentally, a pity that the tremendous influence of the various Christian Churches over the faithful has been inadequately used. The colour problem will be easier of solution if the Churches denounce discrimination, not occasionally, but persistently; and with the same vehemence that is mustered in the denunciation of other social evils like prostitution and crime.

My interest in the colour problem as such was however first aroused after I left school, when I was refused admission to the Colombo Swimming Club several years ago. It was odd that a club in an independent country, and situated opposite 'Temple Trees', the official residence of the Ceylon Prime Minister, was for 'Europeans only'. The authorities concerned had declared that they were merely exercising the democratic right of every association to determine the composition of its membership. An

English friend who belonged to this club was apologetic that the 'democratic right' in practice amounted to the exclusion of coloured persons. This friend's uneasy conscience prompted him to resign from the club. Years later due to public agitation the doors of the club were opened to all races.

It is difficult for a coloured person visiting Britain to bring to bear a fresh mind untouched by the expectation of discrimination. One invariably has preconceived notions about the colour problem here, based mostly on newspaper accounts and ugly incidents reported by returning students and travellers. There is a deplorable tendency among coloured persons to misinterpret the everyday misunderstandings, embarrassments and petty annoyances incidental to social life as acts of discrimination. Unworthy discriminatory motives are therefore sometimes unfairly imputed.

On an unforgettable September morning in 1960 my ship reached Southampton. The solemn greyness of the skies and the austere English landscapes were compensated by the graceful movements of hundreds of seagulls. Standing alone on the deck I watched with amusement these birds at play. A few of these huge white creatures whizzed past my head as though to warn of the approach of 'white man's land!'

The first year in England was spent in Leeds where I followed a full-time course in librarianship. The interesting visits to various types of libraries, though impressive in many respects, revealed a shocking inadequacy in books relating to Eastern life and culture. Rarely were even the best known Oriental philosophers and writers of ancient and modern times represented even in translations. British libraries have a responsible role to play in dispelling ignorance, the parent of racial prejudice, by increasing their intake of books on these subjects.

The first few years in England were smooth sailing. It was not until I started looking out for accommodation and a job in London that the ugly monster of colour prejudice raised its challenging head. Prejudice seemed to be more marked in the older age groups. It would seem that the gradual dissolution of the vast British Empire as a natural historical process was injurious to the national pride of a generation nurtured in the belief that Britain had a moral right to rule the inferior coloured people in Asia and Africa. On one occasion an acquaintance in a train, a veteran of both World Wars, superciliously remarked: 'We civilized you Indians.' I politely admonished that it was never too late in life to study history. The beneficial effects of British rule in Asia are often exaggerated.

The reason for the claim of white supremacy is understandable. In modern times the white races have been outstanding in industrialization, technological advancement and colonialism. Still, this staggering prosperity could not have been achieved without the preceding centuries of man's endeavours in the more ancient countries like China, Egypt and India, or without the slave labour of millions of subject races.

Another glaring example of prejudice occurred when I accidentally trampled the foot of an elderly woman in a London street. My instantaneous apology was ignored and she screamed frantically, 'Coloured Indian bastard!' She could have restricted herself to 'bastard' with perhaps an unprintable Anglo-Saxon four-letter word! Under the circumstances the additional phrase 'coloured Indian' seemed more effective to express her anger. Unfortunately the term 'coloured person' has come to mean 'second-class citizen'. If by 'white' is meant the colour of snow, I have yet to meet a person belonging to the 'white' races. The truth is that every human being is coloured with varying shades and degrees of pigmentation.

In the struggle to find accommodation in London, I ran into several landlords and landladies who profited financially by the existence and maintenance of the colour bar. A case in point was a landlady who, noticing my plight, was willing to let a room at an extra five shillings per week because 'you are a coloured bloke'. She had no convincing explanation to give for what seemed a 'taxation on pigmentation'. Instances of this kind could be multiplied. A fate that clearly emerged was that none of these persons harboured an aversion for coloured persons. They upheld the colour bar for pecuniary motives as against psychological ones. I tried to look at the issue from the angle of a landlord who

I

objected to having coloured tenants for their alleged strange ways of living. What were these strange ways? 'The West Indians had parties', and 'Indian cooking smelled of curry powder.' In this instance the colour bar was the result of frowning at 'un-English behaviour'. An insularity of outlook admits of no deviations from a standardized pattern of life. The West Indian fondness for song, dance and gay abandon is imperceptibly introducing a much wanted element of frolic and relaxation to the rather staid and tense tempo of English life. Is it the haunting suspicion and fear of change in the English character that resists foreign influences? What is objectionable in the aromatic herbal flavour of curry to a nation that does not mind the omnipresent smell of bacon and eggs every morning? The crux of the colour problem could be reduced to three elements which are complementary: the fear of alien influences that might challenge and upset accepted ways of thinking and acting; the smug complacency in tradition; and the disguised sense of superiority which outwardly manifests itself in racial discrimination.

I have sad memories of refusals by landlords, and of accommodation bureaux in London which specialize in letting rooms and flats to 'Europeans only'. Investigations revealed that lodgings were kept unoccupied for months despite the acute housing shortage, until white tenants were found. Certain newspapers unashamedly continue to accept advertisements with the stipulation 'no coloureds' or 'Europeans only'. Solely for the purpose of this essay I explored the extent of the operation of this kind of institutional discrimination by visiting two leading marriage bureaux in London. The official policy in both instances was to turn down applications from coloureds and discourage mixed marriages.

Many persons with whom the subject of mixed marriages was discussed frowned on such unions with no satisfactory explanations to justify their standpoints. Mixed marriages are the best foundations on which to build a world of racial integration. Human beings differ from one another for varying reasons and not merely because of racial differences. Racial differences are insignificant in the face of the most important factor of love and mutual consideration, the presence or absence of which makes or mars a marriage. Since every so-called race was formed by the mixture of other so-called races, there can be no such thing as racial purity. It is paradoxical that educated persons who would readily agree to the preceding statement often blush when, for instance, an African gets married to an English girl.

Condescension, expressed in a thousand subtle ways but difficult to define, together with patronizing, largely constitute the colour bar. The obstacles to finding comfortable lodgings or employment commensurate with one's qualifications are mostly the result of a concealed feeling of contempt for the Coloureds. Occasionally the doors of employment are opened to a coloured worker as though to proclaim to the world an act of Christian charity! Has the coloured worker no equal right to work provided he is suitable? The coloured worker is handicapped by his poor competitive capacity in the labour market: to get a job he must not merely be the equal but also the superior of his rivals. At the outset he encounters prejudice. Whereas the white employee under normal conditions commences work with the underlying assumption on the part of the employer that he will be efficient, the coloured worker is expected to be unequal to his duties. It is usual for any worker to make mistakes during the initial stages of learning a technique. In one of my jobs in London mistakes were too quickly detected and I was upbraided within the first few weeks. The same mistakes of a comparatively new English colleague were overlooked. There were hints of dismissal on the incorrect charges of having been 'slow and inefficient'. For several weeks I went through a stage of agonizing insecurity and sleepless nights. It occurred to me that a change of job was the only solution; but what if every employer acted in the same irrational manner? One's existence as a human being was at stake. Before long it was fairly clear that the only thing against me was the colour of my complexion, for my boss confessed to believing in the insulting generalization that all coloured persons were lazy! A sympathetic girl whispered that everyone in the office save herself had been nasty to a Nigerian girl who had been there before. She added that her colleagues were somewhat subtly hostile to her when she befriended this Nigerian typist.

An impediment to solving the colour problem in Britain is, strangely, the customary politeness of the average Englishman to his neighbours, be they foreign or British. Frankness of expression is not as a rule an outstanding virtue here. The social graces and the calculated minimization and avoidance of friction by not uttering unpleasant statements, the many 'thank-you's' and the profuse apologies, tend to conceal the underlying suspicion of the foreigner. Children are taught to say pleasant things and avoid hurtful remarks however true. Consequently a stranger in Britain, unless he is very alert, might easily misjudge the situation and think that he is received with warmth and friendship everywhere. Since it is un-English to behave rudely to foreigners, the air of artificial cordiality makes it difficult to discover one's genuine friends. It is almost impossible at first to unravel the attitudes of other persons towards oneself. The tensions, jealousies and rivalries get temporarily eclipsed by this veil of artificial goodwill. The feeling of animosity, however, finds an outlet in a crisis such as the Notting Hill riots a few years ago. The situation in Britain might be contrasted with that of a hypothetical society where honest and frank conversation reveals bluntly a dislike of intruding settlers. In such a society it would be easier, first, to recognize the existence of animosity; and second, to take remedial measures.

The problems of race relations may be tackled at several levels. One might strive for integration at the social level by agitation for the removal of all barriers that obstruct Coloureds' entry into clubs, dance floors, restaurants, schools and other places. Economic measures designed to raise living standards might lessen the disparity of real incomes between the poor Coloureds and the rich Whites. Educationally too the gap could be bridged through intensive teaching programmes, adult education, audio-visual means and similar ingenious techniques of imparting information. The raising of economic and educational standards will inevitably improve the social standing of the Coloureds. Still there are the psychological hurdles that Coloureds have to face. A formal social acceptability is insufficient unless accompanied by a positive feeling of companionship.

Equality is a juristic concept, and if the 'equality' of the coloured man in a predominantly white society remains only at the legal level the situation is unsatisfactory. Fundamentally, a lasting solution may be found in uprooting the deeply ingrained psychological animosities rather than in the mere removal of economic and educational handicaps, important though such measures are. The mental association of certain fixed attributes and behaviour patterns with coloured persons is the essence of racialist thinking. It is revealing that the segregationists, such as the upholders of *apartheid*, have a uniform reaction to every coloured person. The colour bar may be removed in multi-racial societies if education, the press, radio and the other media of instruction, stress the supreme importance of an attitude that seeks to evaluate every person, coloured or white, as a distinct and complex individual. The realization of the extraordinary diversity of human types within every racial fold will help to break down long cherished beliefs like 'West Indians are gay', 'Whites are superior', 'Indians are spiritual' and 'Negroes are brutal and sexy'.

A law against racial discrimination is urgently required. Legislation will help to formulate standards: though difficult to enforce, it would be the expressed declaration by the community of what is held to be good and right. The lesson to be learnt from the United States in this matter is the extraordinary power the Federal Government has in the struggle for the achievement of full equality for Negroes through measures such as executive orders, the promotion of civil rights legislation and the institution of desegregation suits. Prejudice generally drags on though its legal and institutional trappings are disappearing. Fierce resistance has to be countered before the democracies of the world become egalitarian in spirit.

The keen rivalry for jobs, particularly during a depression, is a major source of friction in multi-racial societies. The spirit of competition, normal to capitalist economies, takes a racialist turn when Coloureds are viewed as intruders in the traditional homelands of white people. When the grim alternative seems to be starvation coloured minorities tend to accept employment under conditions favourable to the employer such as lower wages, longer hours of work and unpleasant menial tasks. It is not surprising under these circumstances for local workers to complain that their coloured colleagues bring down conditions of work and lower general living standards. Thus an essentially economic rivalry for jobs tends to incite racial animosities. If the economic trends in a crisis are clearly analysed by trade-union leaders, the susceptibility of workers' minds to dangerous racialist interpretations might be minimized if not altogether eliminated. In the sphere of industry the trade unions should adopt a more liberal policy in respect of increasing the coloured membership. The status of the coloured worker might also be improved by the establishment of vocational training centres, particularly because of his poorer chances of obtaining apprenticeship in a society of predominantly white employers.

After the Civil War in the United States when slavery was abolished, the opponents of integration cast doubts upon the Negro's capacity to survive as a free man. Once the opportunity was given the Negro made a substantial contribution to the achievements of American civilization over the last 100 years. The Negro fought back and denied the inferiority that had been attributed to him. Therefore given the opportunities there is great hope in the potentialities of the economically under-developed parts of the world where most of the coloured people live. The stigma of inferiority cast on the underprivileged and undernourished could be erased by lifting living standards.

It is customary to regard the white man as the oppressor and the coloured as the oppressed. After the coloured peoples of the world have established their right to equality, it would be an alarming repetition of history if the white races were subjected to discriminatory humiliation. The coloured person who suffers from a sense of oppression and antipathy towards the white races is just as much responsible for the colour bar as those who overtly discriminate. Hatred breeds hatred and retaliatory measures only add to the existing bitterness. Judging from the vitriolic speeches of certain African nationalists pouring out their inveterate hatred of Europeans, the possibility of a colour bar in reverse is no longer remote. With many African territories becoming independent sovereign states the future of European minorities there is somewhat unsettled. If the European states surrender power gracefully with a resignation to the inevitability of political freedom in these territories, the militant quality of African nationalism may be modified. If the transition of power comes as a matter of course in the constitutional evolution of these nascent states, thereby eliminating the need for a struggle to assert political independence, better race relations will follow. That an enlightened liberalism in these matters characterized British colonial policy in the post-war era is a tribute to the foresight of her statesmen.

These years in England have convinced me that the English people who discriminate constitute a numerically dwindling unintelligent fringe. The harshness of the colour bar has caused in me a softening maturity of outlook so that I deeply sympathize with the plight of people anywhere who are persecuted, suppressed or downtrodden. I have come to view the race problem in a wider perspective: race seems only one of the innumerable barriers, such as political frontiers and social divisions, that divide men—the aching divisions of our time that are no less appalling than colour discrimination itself.

10

Indifference

ADIL JUSSAWALLA

India

Adil Jussawalla was born in 1940 in India. He published a book of poems in 1962, and wrote some plays before that. He studied architecture for one year in London. At present he is at University College, Oxford, and is reading English Language and Literature. He hopes to freelance and/or teach in London after obtaining his degree in Oxford.

> We were not told to aspire to exellence;
> We were asked to make peace with mediocrity—
> JAMES BALDWIN, *The Fire Next Time*

To have learnt how to make a virtue of bitterness; to have witnessed the increasing despair of one's coloured friends; to have seen some of them driven to violence, one almost to murder, knowing that all one's capacity for love, then, is incapable of easing the pain accompanying the drop and smash of their careers; to have heard of cases of suicide and insanity among coloured students here; to have endured the steady disavowal of one's national identity in the face of an indifference which is more ambiguous, more thorough and more skilfully underplayed than conscious discrimination; to have felt one's capacity for love gradually being replaced by an increasingly bitter helplessness, at times becoming an indiscriminate and murderous hate against all white authority, till it seems that all Whites are engaged in a conspiracy of silence against the coloured—this was not what a foreign education meant to me when I was a student in Bombay.

Nothing in my education or my family background had prepared me for this great mortuary of indifference every foreigner
finds himself trapped in during his first few years here; nothing
really could have, because no one had told me that I was, because
of the way I looked or spoke or laughed, an inferior person; as the
very cosmopolitan nature of the city and my school was an
effective antidote to whatever racial and colour prejudices exist
in India. English boys, Anglo-Indians, Russians, Jews, and later
Americans studied with us, and though there was some mud-
slinging and name-calling during the troubled days before and
after Independence, there was little conscious grouping together
to the exclusion of one or other community on grounds of colour.

Towards the end of our school careers, Britain, for many of us,
was the logical end of our formal education, so anglicized as to
lay greater stress on Lancashire cotton-industries, the Elizabethans,
the Corn Laws, than on anything the Indian peoples had achieved
in the past, or were likely to in the future. Many of us would
dearly have liked to continue studying in Britain, if only because
it meant freedom from one's parents, a room of one's own, sex.

At seventeen, I came over believing in my gifts, my ability to
absorb, build, be assimilated by society here; later, perhaps, to
return, as a better person, capable of leading a better life than, I
felt then, India would let me lead.

At twenty-three, I find most British attempts at friendship
disingenuous; think most jokes involving Negroes, darkies and
wogs are tasteless; regard most failures to get a room as a deliberate slight, and whenever there's talk of British justice, law and
order I pretend I'm not listening.

Though in my own case all this has little to do with my being
coloured, since I do not normally pass as coloured, nor, often, as
an Indian, six years in Britain have made any pretence at a cool
approach to the colour problem impossible.

This essay, then, is really an attempt to define the colour
problem as felt or witnessed, mainly in London. That the problem
is a very different one for the coloured man himself, and that it
can't be solved by the white man alone needs no emphasis. And
for most in Britain it is no problem at all.

I think it is true to say that the lowest denominator all the coloured peoples of the world have in common is subjugation; and I don't think coloured people can forget it easily. It is hard for the coloured to forget that they have been attacked, used and discarded by the Whites—in the East and the West, and that most of them now, for better or for worse, are under the long-term dominance of Western technocrats.

But Independence and the freed peoples' right to choose their lives have also increased a very live though unspecified fear in an ex-Empire like Britain that the very instruments it used to 'civilize' the coloured—arms, propaganda, literacy—are being turned to ends radically alien to Britain's; they have made the British uneasy living with immigrants of races they are unused to treating as equals, ignored and disregarded among peoples they were once very superior to and upset by ways of living they have no taste for. And this fear, this unease, is, at last, forcing widespread dislikes and prejudices into focus and exploding from within the structure of British society itself, such myths as British racial tolerance, justice, etc.

If the British were ever tolerant of foreigners on their own shores (being notoriously intolerant of them abroad) it was because they had nothing to lose. They were in a ruthlessly powerful position where they could be sanctimonious, make concessions, entertain their subjects lavishly—particularly those wealthy colonials it paid to entertain—and be liked for it. Now, with an Empire lost, with the coloured population of Britain rising, though still a ludicrous one per cent. of the entire population, discrimination is open, violent and bloody—the Notting Hill riots in 1958 being only a symptom of unrecorded currents of violence running through Britain's bigger cities today—from unprovoked attacks on 'darkies' in factories to a smouldering resentment at their gayer and noisier lives.

What I am trying to say is that though, intellectually, some citizens of this country recognize the extent of their past colonial folly, recognize the need to tolerate, if not to accept, the coloured, they have been through no collective emotional crisis, no comparable degradation to enable them to feel any more sympathetic towards their hopes, their ambitions, their constant striving for a communal identity than they used to. 'Britons never shall be slaves' is a refrain charged with *hubris* at the best of times, but when sung loudly, proudly and a little tunelessly in the pit of the Albert Hall, is to an outsider also a nastily overplayed theme.

Though, in theory, many intellectuals are liberals by temperament, or extremely left-wing politically, in practice they retain most of a vague, imperfectly-understood national conservatism, and the regenerative value of Britain in relation to its colonies, ex-colonies and underdeveloped countries is barely questioned.

In short, the mentality that produced the two-faced Hastings, outwardly so kind to Indians, privately so vicious; the mentality that produced a Cornwallis or a General Dyer (*I wanted to teach them a lesson they would never forget*), the mentality of the professional civilizer and the 'civilized' professional carrying the cross of his faith to those less-fortunate races he would like to make his burden, is still the predominant one here and has not changed appreciably sixteen years after the Empire lost its first fatal hunk, India.

And, to be fair to the citizens of Britain, how could it have changed, when no significant reorientation is being attempted in the schools and universities here; how can it change—the mentality itself being the product of more than four centuries of Western adventure and loot in the East and Africa, and many more centuries of hatred and war between the Christian countries and the pagan ones, of conscious mis-education, wilful distortion of facts, as can be seen from the hideous letters and journals of not a few British civil servants and their wives in the last century?

For the coloured student, the coloured immigrant, the position would seem hopeless, because he has to bear the brunt not only of his own mistakes in a foreign country, but of the mistakes of any individual here who happens to be coloured; he is responsible not only for his own actions but for his past in relation to a master-race which still sees him through its own glass of history, darkly, not sufficiently differentiated from the coloured mass for him to begin existing as an individual who suffers, is hungry, loves and dies like any of its members.

What is to be done, the British ask, to make his position better here?

Since it is the problem of the coloured man as a foreigner that is being dealt with, it might be worthwhile touching on the complicated world of the foreigner in Britain first.

Insularity, and a sense of having powerful neighbours has made an extreme defensiveness, a fixed and irrational xenophobia part of the climate of Britain for centuries. This xenophobia is attested to not by the coloured peoples alone but by visitors from Europe and the United States as well. This xenophobia, when working against coloured peoples, is strengthened by dissimilarities in manner, speech, dress and above all appearance.

Every foreigner, when he enters Britain, has to remember he is under suspicion, and so will be treated with irony, condescension or worse, and the coloured man, however adaptable he may have become during the course of his stay here, will find himself excluded from the commerce of people of a status and background similar to his own.

Every coloured immigrant has to remember that whatever his background, education and achievement in his home country, the moment he steps ashore here, he is part of that misunderstood, misrepresented, and misled mass of disinhabited strays who have fringed the British consciousness for several decades now, but have never been important to it.

If he is Indian or Pakistani, he is part of that coloured tribe that lives squalidly twelve to a room, because there is no better place for him, and most of the better rooms he applies for are mysteriously taken.

If he is a West Indian or an African he will have to put up with a murderous sex-envy, scandals concerning his private life and obscene myths concerning his background.

In short, no coloured man can live in Britain for long without realizing that in spite of all the social advantages he enjoys along with the non-coloured population—National Health, Government Assistance, etc.—he is the lowest-graded citizen in the country, and that the social advantages he dreamt of in his home are not only not forthcoming, but that most doors, normally open to him there, are very simply, very gently, but very firmly shut. Should he abandon even the hope of a successful career—and I mean not as a student, but as one trying to advance in the more competitive world of business, of medicine, of art, of the factory, and concentrate on living less ambitiously—he is surrounded by vague hostilities which daily threaten to break his confidence in his neighbours if not himself, so that to make himself understood to the citizens here is an attempt of appalling magnitude. This is because their cultural direction is now away from, not towards him, is technological not humanistic; away from his past and into a future where his past is less interesting as a complex in time than its mathematical function as a digit, a symbol, an integer among several dealing with incomes, *per capita* increases, steel production, food surpluses.

What hope is there for the coloured man ever to share a country well with a white man, other than through 'making peace with mediocrity' (James Baldwin's words)? How is he to 'aspire to excellence' without becoming, on the way, a neurotic, a saint, an ape, or a criminal?

The speeding dawn of technology has separated great numbers in the West and East from a sense of time, a sense of continuity, a sense of the past, the irony of it being that though the white man feels supremely able to emerge from his night, no coloured man is allowed to feel that he can ever emerge from his. And where the average Britisher has been given plenty of fodder from his colonial past to help him face his future with confidence, smothering himself with a kind of historical amnesia, in his increasingly depersonalized environment, the very hope of the coloured man rests on his being able to give meaning and dignity to his.

One thing is quite clear. However hard the British try to forget the squalor and waste caused by colonialism, race, and colour prejudices, which, in some cases, verge on the pathological, coloured people can't let them forget it now. They have lost too much, too often, too unequally.

For the next few decades, I think, British intellectuals are going to be harassed by awkward questions they haven't asked themselves yet and which the coloured people are only just demanding an answer to. It has become surprisingly easy for the young British intellectual to be indignant over Auschwitz, the Nazis, lynchings in the American South, without being concerned at the misfortune to which his kind of education and consciousness submitted peoples from all over the world, and the atrocities his rulers and his armies committed on them and, perhaps, still do commit for his sake.

He says he is angry. He says he would like to help. But how much does he care to teach himself, first of all, of the history of his emotional attitude to other races; and of the emotional climate that has helped create and spread the dreadful tensions between white and coloured, East and West, Christian and non-Christian today?

It seems ludicrous that the peoples of the East, the peoples of backward nations, of small nations, should train millions of their young people in technologies and sciences originating in Britain, and the young British remain so indifferent to them as people.

If an Indian child, say, spends years acquiring an elementary knowledge of physics, is it too much to ask that a British child be instructed in attitudes that will not degrade him should he come here to continue his studies?

When I was a child, on my way to my aunt's house, I would sometimes see a group of very beautiful children, dirty, unkempt, living in a shattered little garage by the road. But they were blond. Each time I passed them I wondered who they were, for it seemed a mistake, a reversal of the order I was accustomed to, that blond children should be living in such conditions, staring quietly and emptily at those who went past. I had seen no blonde people living in such conditions before.

I did not know then that there were, perhaps, thousands of such illegitimate children in the country, left by the war, soldiers, hunger, rape.

To me now they are a symbol of just those kinds of transformations that are to be lived with and loved when race mixes with race, race conquers race, race outcasts race, and the word 'home' for millions of displaced people in the West and the East has become an uncertain and often desperate jibe.

They lived wretchedly. But few people who had seen them could forget them. They represented a kind of injustice (or justice if you like) which was upsetting perhaps because no one felt they could do very much to help them or even wanted to.

In Britain, the children's situation is reversed and the position of coloured adults more ambiguous. There is squalor and there are people living in it obviously different from the main body of people here. They would like to help themselves, but the odds are enormous, often hopelessly so. They suffer from a long tradition of being oppressed, the British from a long tradition of being the oppressors. Both are uneasily conscious that while the past can be forgotten for a few years, the solution to their problems doesn't lie in forgetting their origins there.

Perhaps education will not solve the problem; perhaps what is needed is the collective emotional crisis mentioned earlier, through events beyond the control of both the Whites and the coloured. But if the British cannot learn to live with other races, cannot accept the coloured among them, they continue an internationally anomalous and, essentially, self-injurious tradition— that of being anti-colour, anti-East, anti-big-nation, anti-little-nation, anti-everything but a sick longing for lost power, unable to lose well, and unable, after a period of Empire, to get used to the sense of their country's historical limits, and the hard work involved in loving races no better or worse than them—though very different.

The test of Little England succeeding where Great Britain failed is whether, at last, it has the courage to take the hard road that leads to accepting other races with a certain tolerance, love, and grace.

Epilogue

THE essays presented in these pages stand in their own right as a body of commentary on race prejudice by those who are best placed to know its consequences. But it may be useful to summarize the themes and attitudes which emerge from all the essays submitted for the competition, whether they are included in this volume or not. It is not possible to do justice in a few pages to the richness of material contained in over seventy essays, some of which were very long, some of a highly personal nature, some sophisticated, some naïve, and written from so many diverse backgrounds. It seemed to us that the least defective mirror of what was expressed would be an account based in some measure on a descriptive analysis of the content of the essays. The general lines of this content analysis (which did not include the essays written by women, as there were so few of them) were determined by the form which the students were invited to adopt when writing the essays (see Preface).

We received seventy-three essays, of which sixty-eight were written by men and five by women. Table 1 summarizes the information about the men, Table 2 that on the women. In Table 3 we set out

TABLE I

ESSAYS WRITTEN BY MEN

Country of origin	Number of essays	Institutions		Courses	
		Universities	Colleges of technology	Humanities	Science
Nigeria	23	13	10	13	10
West Indies	9	6	3	7	2
India	7	5	2	6	1
Uganda	5	2	3	5	–
Ceylon	4	2	2	3	1
Sierra Leone	3	3	–	3	–
Ghana	3	–	3	2	1
Kenya	2	2	–	1	1
Sudan	2	2	–	2	–
South Africa	2	1	1	1	1
Pakistan	2	1	1	1	1
Malaya	1	1	–	1	–
Indonesia	1	1	–	1	–
British Guiana	1	–	1	1	–
Saudi Arabia	1	–	1	1	–
Tanganyika	1	1	–	1	–
Somalia	1	1	–	1	–
Totals	68	41	27	50	18

separately further information about the African, Asian and West Indian groups of men. The distribution of groups by area of origin shows a preponderance of essays from Africa; this reflects the current trends in the student population. The distribution by institution is reasonably representative but, as one would expect, there is a strong

TABLE 2

ESSAYS WRITTEN BY WOMEN

Country of origin	Institution	Subject
Kenya (Indian parentage)	Cambridge	History
India	Oxford	P.P.E.
India	London, Institute of Education	Education
Cuba (Jamaican parentage)	London, Institute of Education	Education
Trinidad	Oxford	Modern History; Social and Administrative Studies

TABLE 3

DISTRIBUTION OF MEN BY AREA OF ORIGIN

	Number	Average age, years	Average time spent in Britain, years	Average length of planned sojourn in Britain, years
Africa	42	29·2	2·6	4·7
Asia	16	29·3	2·3	4·2
West Indies and British Guiana	10	24·7	2·3	4·5
Total group	68	28·5	2·4	4·5

bias towards students of humanities. The ratio is 1 : 2·78 in their favour, while for all overseas students listed by the British Council (1962) attending universities and colleges of technology, the ratio is 1 : 0·68 in favour of the sciences. The average ages of the African and Asian students are similar, but the age of the West Indian group is much lower. This might possibly be related to the nature of the West Indian educational system. The average age of 28·5 years for the whole group is rather high: this is partly explained by the large proportion of post-graduate students in the group.

Table 4 on page 138 summarizes the information about authors of the essays selected for publication.

The content analysis of the essays followed the lines of the broad categories implicit in the terms of the competition.

(a) Experience of the colour problem before arrival in this country: the intention was to include here views, attitudes, and personal experiences concerning Europeans and the image of Britain. However, the content of the essays forced an extension of this to other aspects of inter-group relations at home, such as tribalism, racialism, relations between social classes, etc.

(b) Experience in Britain: this was concerned with the writers' first impressions and their immediate responses; with experience of prejudice and discrimination in personal relations; and with such matters as social class, religion, education, lodgings, work, organizations, other national groups, etc.

(c) Changes in attitude occurring during the visit to Britain.

TABLE 4

AUTHORS OF THE PUBLISHED ESSAYS

Name	Country of origin	University or college	Courses
Syed Ali Baquer	India	Oxford	Social and Administrative Studies
Elliott Bastien	Trinidad	Birmingham	Petroleum Production Engineering
S. K. Dabo	Sierra Leone	Hull, Oxford	Comparative Literature
Francis M. Deng.	Sudan	London	Law
Chikwendu Nwariaku	Nigeria	Newcastle-on-Tyne	Civil Engineering
Patricia Madoo	Trinidad	Oxford	History; Social and Administrative Studies
Mervyn E. Morris*	Jamaica	Oxford	English
Adil Jussawalla	India	Oxford	English
Kenneth Ramchand	Trinidad	Edinburgh	English
S. Weeraperuma	Ceylon	Leeds	Librarianship

PRIOR EXPERIENCE

The surveys carried out by P.E.P. (1955) and Carey (1956) have shown that the adaptation of students to the British society and to its educational institutions is considerably influenced by the country of origin, language, culture, social structure, previous experience of Europeans—and the shade of skin. The P.E.P. survey, for example, reported that less than half of the light-skinned West Indian students experienced discrimination in Britain as compared with 80 per cent. of dark-skinned West Indians and 72 per cent. of Africans. Only about a third of students from Asian and Mediterranean countries reported experiences of discrimination. But it remains true that colour is by no means the only variable affecting students' adaptation. For example, in a recent

* Author of the prize-winning essay

book on Indian students in Britain, Singh (1963) describes some fairly startling differences in their reactions to this country and in the patterns of adaptation to it related to the social background of the students.

Some of these various background factors were quite clearly reflected in the essays. The determination of views held at home about Britain is complex and often results in ambivalence. But the nature of this ambivalence varies with the nature of the problems encountered at home. Thus, many of the West Indians are thoroughly confused on coming to Britain by the natives' inability to discriminate between finer shades of colour. The crude categorization into 'white' and 'black' or 'coloured' seems to them to miss the finer points of distinction so common in the West Indies. One student writes: 'In the West Indies we find an amazing double vision. For, in contemplation of human groups, no society has developed a more delicate instrument of perception. Coming to Britain is like entering a land where the natives suffer from a peculiar kind of colour blindness. . . .' More detailed consideration of this subtle meaning of shade in relation to social status in the West Indies will be found in some of the essays.

It is interesting, perhaps, to add that the theme of the belief in the inherent superiority of light shades of skin appears also in some essays which are not from the West Indies. This is, for example, a generalized conclusion reached by a student from India, a woman: 'I understand that it is human nature to appreciate fairness of complexion, and hence each race tries to prove its superiority over others from this point of view. When one is bound to admit one's inferiority, one tries to subdue this inferiority complex by show of hatred towards the privileged opponent.'

But this is hardly typical of Indian attitudes towards colour. And just as the background of the Indian student differs enormously from that of the West Indian, so is the previous experience of the colour problem different for the West Africans on the one hand, and for the East, Central, and South Africans on the other. The presence of large groups of Europeans and Asians has complicated racial issues and created stormy paths to independence in East and Central Africa. Here is, for example, a view from Uganda: 'To the European, the African was an ignorant person deserving education only to become an obedient servant; the Indian was another of those primitive savages. To the Indian, the European was an inevitable but hateable proud master, and the African a primitive native only worthy of exploiting. To the African, the European was an unavoidable, pompous and sometimes brutal master who, though clever and sometimes useful, must be driven out at the earliest possible opportunity.'

It is hardly worth repeating that these views are not necessarily representative. It remains true, however, that in West Africa the same racial issues have not arisen; there have been no European settlers and very few Asians. Thus, the West African students' experience of Europeans has been limited mainly to their role as administrators, teachers, missionaries, medical officers, &c. One should add immediately that this does not necessarily ease the path of the West African student's adjustment to this country: he has a longer way to go to come to terms with the colour problem in Britain.

Experience of non-settler Europeans reflected in the essays strikes a favourable balance. Of the 52 instances in which this experience is explicitly referred to, 38 are highly or moderately favourable. But of these favourable mentions, nearly half (17) refer to missionaries and teachers—with only one strong expression of disapproval towards a teacher in a mission school. The other categories of Europeans (such as district commissioners, civil servants, medical officers, &c.) are much more evenly distributed in the general range which varies from extremely favourable (14) through favourable (24) to unfavourable (4) and frankly bad (10). One of the results of these relatively favourable experiences is an increased sensitivity to what happens on arrival in Britain. As one Nigerian student put it: '. . . The people encountered in the United Kingdom differ a great deal from the former colonial masters.' In the context of the essay, the implication was that prejudice and discrimination in Britain were much worse than was to be expected on the basis of experiences at home, in Nigeria. And another: 'West Africans find it difficult to appreciate the implications of the colour bar . . . unlike the black South Africans, the East Africans and the American Negroes, they have lived in a homogeneous if not completely free society.'

Colour and race loom large in the instances of various inter-group conflicts or difficulties at home which the essays mentioned. In the total of thirty-three cases which explicitly refer to various conflicts, no less than nineteen are concerned with skin colour or variations on this theme. But reflections on the universal nature of inter-group prejudice transcending colour and manifesting itself in a number of forms (religion, class, caste, tribe) are by no means absent. One of the students writes: '. . . It is difficult to conceive of a country where one will not encounter racialism in one form or another . . . even as a child in the Sudan I saw the reactions of one tribe to another, of one ethnic group to others, and, of course, the attitudes of foreign races towards our own.' An Indian writes: '. . . It is essential to grasp that it is not white men *only* who are inclined to this particular type of mistake.'

It is, however, the inclination of the white men to commit 'this particular type of mistake' which is the writers' preoccupation within the framework set by the essay competition. According to the retrospective evidence present in the essays, there is a keen awareness before leaving home of the racist tendencies in the world of the white man. 'Events in Alabama, Notting Hill, Sophia and Moscow are an eloquent testimony to the fact that the problem cuts across ideological and regional boundaries,' writes one of the students. In this context South Africa is mentioned more frequently than any other country (twenty-two mentions) but it is closely followed by the United States (eighteen mentions).

Though we are not concerned in this section with students' experiences on arrival in Britain, one effect of South African background on the first reactions to this country should perhaps be presented at this point: 'I realized the indescribable human indignity [at home] . . . to breathe the air, to be able to go to any place I pleased, to talk to anyone I chose, to find the London policeman a friend . . . I was worth my qualifications and paid my worth, not a percentage of a white man's pay . . . I re-evaluated the Europeans.'

And here is, like a mirror image, the beginning of another essay from South Africa (which was not submitted for the competition):

For much of my thinking life the question of colour has obsessed me. It has forced moral issues on me which I have been unable to resolve; it has demanded sacrifices of me which I have not always been prepared to make; it has nibbled at my conscience and eaten into my self-respect; it has distorted my social values, it has estranged me from my own community and, finally, it has driven me from my own country. For I am an African born and bred—but a pink one from South Africa.

The concluding paragraph of this essay provides a counterpart to the one just quoted:

I have not met many coloured people in Britain—very few in fact. But I feel cured of a sickness I contracted in early childhood. I don't feel the compulsion to seek out the black face at a party and be nice to it and to demonstrate to it that I am with it all the way. Occasionally though I have relapses when I feel constrained to excuse myself to those whom I suppose to be free of this contamination: this is where these confessions of a colour addict began.

The race problem in the United States is also a salient point of the image of the 'white man's world'. The frequent mention of the United States in terms of racialism is an indication of this general awareness. One Nigerian student commenting on America's role in the world today writes that 'social conscience is much more developed and sustained in Britain than in America. And today nothing has so singularly challenged America's claim to world leadership as the clumsy and dastardly approach to the Negro problem'. This is a fair representation of the views of others who referred to this issue. However, one also meets frequent acknowledgements of the efforts being made in the United States to deal with the problem, and a realization that there is a continuous, if slow, trend towards improvement.

Other 'white' countries are not frequently mentioned; but the rare references to Australia (three times) are all in terms of restrictive immigration laws, the white Australia policy, and the lack of full citizenship for the Australian aboriginals; to Portugal (also three times) in terms of discrimination in the colonies; to Russia (twice) in relation to the recent disturbances. The Scandinavian countries are referred to, and so is France, in both cases for an explicit denial of the existence of the cruder forms of colour discrimination.

How does Britain fare? In order to answer this, a tally was made of 'ideas held about Britain before arrival' in terms of their evaluative content. Of the 46 relevant statements concerning 'the country and the people', 20 were definitely favourable, 21 fairly non-committal and only 5 definitely unfavourable. This distribution is approximately paralleled by the distribution of views held before arrival concerning the colour problem in Britain. Of forty-four statements made, 16 confessed to having thought that there was no colour problem here, 21 were not very sure one way or the other, and 7 were expecting to find on arrival an extensive colour problem.

Some students complained that the image of Britain projected at home does not prepare them for what they find here on arrival. This is due in part to the over-optimistic accounts of those who return: 'When the sophisticated been-to's returned to West Africa they concerned themselves with the delights of the mother country and neglected the colour problem,' complains a student from Sierra Leone. Also, lectures and courses tend to display the official brand of optimism: 'In Nigeria cultural organizations usually arrange a series of lectures for students going overseas to acquaint them with the way of life—none of the speakers made even a passing reference to the colour problem.'

It appears that in some cases these idealized accounts do no more than confirm information previously received. In Tanganyika, writes a student, 'all along at school we are shown a number of films depicting life in Britain. The British Council and the American Information Services have been the chief agencies for this. Most of these films have shown life in the West at its best: model schools, welfare services, new towns, technical achievements, scientific and medical progress. All these have tended to support current ideas held by African school-children about life in Britain. Ignorance about Europeans, the propaganda of the films, and the publications of the British information office all combine to bring about this illusive picture of Britain. And this is the root of the problem facing the new student in Britain. One soon discovers that the imagined conception is far from reality. Most of the ideals previously held about Britain are gradually discarded.'

In the next two sections we have attempted to summarize, as far as was possible, the ways in which these 'ideals' were 'gradually discarded', the experience which led to the changes of attitudes and to the emergence of attitudes held after some years of study in Britain.

EXPERIENCE IN BRITAIN

I have often had occasion to remark that much of the nationalism of the West Indian Negro is born at Paddington, the train station at which I arrived when I came first to England. After a tiring two weeks at sea and a five-hour train ride in from Plymouth one awakes to the scurryings of white porters who not only seem eager to carry one's bags—but are extremely deferential. Little do the porters know what an impact they make on coloured immigrants. The average non-student immigrant will perhaps not have been addressed as 'Sir' very often in his life. And he will most certainly not have seen so many white men doing this type of work before. This last goes for West Indian immigrants of all classes. The educated West Indian, in between spells of bewilderment caused by such an impressive novelty as the London Underground, is likely to be somewhat amused too at the accents of the people round about him. He is naturally surprised to find that he speaks English better than a large percentage of Englishmen. He suddenly feels a great sense of pity for so many countrymen at home who for centuries have been fed the picture of the ideal Englishman, and he desires beyond all else that they should share his experience; if he happens to be a believer in the myth of white supremacy, he is almost suddenly emancipated. As he drives through the streets of Paddington he thinks how much better for the English stereotype it would have been if he had been landed in Trafalgar Square in the midst of bowler hats and brollies that he had so often been shown on newsreels. For the first time he is aware of the effectiveness of selective news reporting. He begins to wonder if he has not been falsely led to believe that his fellow Negroes in Africa have not progressed beyond the shanties and tribal dance displays that so often greet him at the cinema. When he later meets Africans who are cultured and sophisticated, when he learns that there are impressive buildings in Accra and Lagos of which he has possibly not heard at home, he wonders why all this information has never been put over to him before. He concludes—perhaps rashly—that there were forces at work in the world at large which were doing everything to set up the association between blackness and poverty, backwardness and savagery, and realizes that he had been beguiled into regarding himself as inferior to the white man—though perhaps only slightly so—simply because there was this false consolation that way out there in the darkness of Africa there were men vastly inferior to himself. In his new mood of enlightenment he is very likely to become hypersensitive, to look for discrimination and to find it both where it exists and where it does not. The English, he had been told, are, unlike the Americans, 'above colour prejudice, their long dealings with the Commonwealth have broadened them and given them experience of many nations and many colours'. He is soon disillusioned about this last. The milling masses of Englishmen round about him are neither broadminded nor experienced in the affairs of other nations, and though no one has made a move to lynch him he is convinced that the staring eyes around him suggest that he should not be in England where 'he is likely to lower their standard of living and to debase their stock'. These English, he feels, are *vis-à-vis* colour prejudice more subtle than the Americans but their methods of expressing disapproval are, if anything, even more psychologically devastating. Of course he is in no condition to distinguish between those who are prejudiced and those who are having the bewildering experience of seeing their first black man off-screen.

This is one account of first impressions on arrival. There is a quality of shock to some of them, of relief to others. All in all, the balance is not unfavourable and it is compounded of a selective and complex variety of images. Most of the West Indians, about half the Africans, and about a quarter of the Asians like what they see on arrival. Definite disappointment is not expressed by any of the West Indians, only by a fifth of the Africans and a quarter of the Asians. Others reserve judgement. Several of the students are pleased with the manner of treatment accorded to them by the immigration officers, some delight in the lack of discrimination in the coaches at the airport, or respond enthusiastically to the pleasantness of the air hostesses; one remembers clearly the impression made on him by the fact that a taxi-driver 'called me Sir'; another noticed with approval some mixed couples in the street.

At the other end of the range, the English climate is responsible for a good deal of initial misery: 'Cold, miserable and wet'; 'Britain is grey and unfriendly' (this is obviously not just climate). There are complaints of loneliness on arrival, of lack of Christian virtues in a country which teaches them abroad, and a number of more general statements about Britain not being 'up to expectations'. In view of the sort of expectations (described in the previous section) that have often been built up, this is less than surprising.

For quite a number of students, the surprise of seeing Europeans working at manual tasks had immediate and stimulating effects on morale. This is clearly expressed in the extract from the essay quoted above. This is also the immediate—and in some cases unforgettable—introduction to the realities of social class structure in Britain, the discovery to many that thinking of 'Whites' as one undifferentiated category cannot fit the realities of their new and complex environment. It is a curious reversal: the British can be so different in so many respects from each other; yet, on the basis of the one and unique clumsy criterion of skin colour, *they* tend to lump together so many people who differ even more from each other. This leads many students to the discovery of a new and wider identity defined through the initially unacceptable criteria imposed by the surrounding society—a discovery which has its powerful consequences.

Sensitivity to class differences in Britain is expressed in quite a number of essays. 'Seeing that the English people are not equal themselves, do I aspire to be equal to an Englishman? If so, what class of Englishman?'—asks a Nigerian. In general, it is found that people at the lower end of the socio-economic ladder tend to be friendlier than those higher up with whom, some students complain, they have little contact. One of them refers to the 'class of Britons that make friends with coloured immigrants most genuinely—from the lower strata of society, that is those who themselves know what it is to be subjected to any form of indignity; he who is down fears no fall, but this class has intellectual limitations'. At the same time, 'the more secure middle and upper strata of British society', writes another, 'lose no time in condemning race prejudice in the lower class. Why can't they set an example by opening their own doors to those middle and upper middle classes of non-Whites?'

These quotations are interesting not only because of the class consciousness that they themselves display; they represent one more expression of the yearning that is perhaps one of the most pervasive characteristics of the essays: to be recognized as an individual and treated as such, to be recognized as having an existence separate from that of 'black' or 'coloured' or whatever. It can be seen in several essays that many of the well-intentioned gestures of acceptance or goodwill flounder because they carry the implication that all coloured students are categorized as a uniform mass. The Nigerian, Indian, West Indian, Ghanaian or any other student does not wish people to be nice to him because he is 'black', and therefore needs support. They wish to enter into individual relations with individuals where each man stands for himself whatever his label.

But instead of this, most of them find evidence of prejudice and discrimination. Sixty-six statements explicitly referring to this have been isolated in the course of the content analysis. Of these, twenty-two report prejudice of extreme or considerable intensity. The incidents vary in nature, and encompass the usual range: difficulty in obtaining lodgings; not being served in hotels; people who avoid sitting next to a coloured man in trains or even in church; milkmen who refuse to deliver; overcharging by taxi drivers; being called a 'nigger bastard', &c. Similar incidents are also reported in the mentions of experiences of prejudice or discrimination found in the content analysis which could be classified as less extreme. Finally, eight statements were found in the essays in which an explicit denial was made of having encountered personally any form of hostile behaviour. Three of these referred to experiences in colleges or universities.

Altogether, concrete instances of hostile behaviour taking various forms are reported by sixty out of the sixty-eight men who sent in essays. The pattern is not particularly consistent, and does not allow any definite statement (if only because of small numbers) about the differences between the groups with regard to their impression of the intensity of the experience. It is difficult to distinguish in reading the essays between those reports of hostile behaviour which are based on genuine hostile intent and those which may well be due to the sensitivity of the writer, between discrimination which is real and that which is imagined. Some of our writers are well aware of this. For example, a Nigerian student comments about one of his compatriots: 'He would complain most bitterly that the attitude of British girls was far from encouraging. But I have personal knowledge that his fortunes at home were no better.' Interpretations of attitudes of others as hostile are determined not only by the objective situation and by the background experiences which have already been discussed, but also by the personality characteristics of those who report them. This too is seen quite clearly by some of our writers, such as the student from Sierra Leone who states flatly, if perhaps a little dogmatically, that 'the reaction to prejudice depends on the personality'. But some of the subtler links between impressions of hostility and personal attitudes are also stated: 'It is precisely those of my Nigerian colleagues apparently most injured by the experience of colour prejudice who utter most wicked and damaging remarks on West Indians.'

Before proceeding to a brief review of the various aspects of their lives which, the students felt, were affected by the hostile attitudes surrounding them, it may be worthwhile to consider their views about the causes of these attitudes. The view that prejudice is a universal phenomenon and that today's attitudes of the white towards the black are caused by a multitude of historical, political, social, and economic factors in addition to the inherence of prejudice in human nature appears in many versions. But sometimes more specific points are made. Several writers feel that some of the difficulty can be attributed to the 'culture shock' felt on both sides when the student arrives in Britain. Specific economic and political issues are also mentioned. One writer, for example, attributes some at least of the difficulty in finding lodgings to political manipulation surrounding the general housing shortage: 'Coloured immigrants are being made scapegoats for the Government's failure to solve its housing problem, and the victims of social distress are made to appear as the causes of it.' Or, in relation to employment: 'Most factory workers on seeing a coloured worker become hostile and nasty, not because they are colour conscious but because they are a threat to their economic position . . . if they later realize the new employee is a student on vacation, they become more friendly.'

A good deal of attention is also paid to the support that prevailing stereotypes find in mass media of communication, advertising, education, &c. Many well-known examples are quoted and there would be no purpose in enumerating them here again. But less obvious instances are also pointed to with some bitterness. Why, asks a student from Nigeria, do so many campaigns concerned with relief from hunger 'choose the coloured man as a symbol of hunger . . . when much of the money is spent on white refugees?' Professor Trevor-Roper's well-known statement about African history comes in for some unflattering comment in at least three essays. One attempt of a student from Uganda to counteract images created by the reading of comics seems worth reporting. He tried to deal with the firm conclusion reached by some children in Edinburgh that, looking as he does, he must be a spaceman. He said he was an African, 'but they refused to believe me. So I told them I was an Englishman but that I had fallen through the chimney—this answer seemed satisfactory.'

Even a brief glance at many essays would reveal the widespread bitterness and disappointment caused by the difficulties in obtaining lodgings and in keeping them. This theme appears in no less than fifty-two essays, with only five students stating explicitly that they had no difficulties. To many this is a stumbling block in achieving a reasonably happy adaptation to life in this country, and it is hardly possible to exaggerate the immense impact that landladies have on the image of Britain that the students will take back with them, and presumably share with others.

The experience of discrimination and restriction is shared by all the three groups of our writers without any hint from the restricted number of cases available that any one of the groups fares better than any other. Twenty-three students report extreme or considerable difficulties which range from the experience of confronting a complete colour bar in seeking accommodation to restrictions imposed on the lodgers once accommodation is found. Twenty-nine students report difficulties of a similar nature though in milder terms.

When considering some of the incidents mentioned, it is possible to come to the conclusion that sometimes the writers may be attributing to colour discrimination restrictions that could have been imposed by some landladies on any lodger (e.g. no girl friend allowed in, no locking of bedroom when having visitors, &c.). It is fully possible that such hypersensitivity exists in many cases; but this is hardly relevant to the problem. Once someone has gone from house to house, from advertisement to advertisement, finding in place after place the incontrovertible evidence of 'no Blacks' 'no Coloured' or of some even more distasteful politer version, it is not surprising that suspicions are aroused and intentions of discrimination sometimes imputed when they do not exist. And then, objectively, there is the 'colour tax': in order to obtain accommodation, the students must frequently pay more than the normal rates or accept lodgings in sub-standard areas. Carey wrote in 1956 that 'colour tax is a process by which the coloured student gets second-rate accommodation, second-rate jobs, and second-rate girlfriends—"second-rate" in the sense that they are of a standard not normally acceptable to British students.' He goes on: 'Colour-tax is symptomatic of the half-way house in which the coloured people find themselves here; a situation that is neither full acceptance, nor out-right rejection, but limited social participation: acceptance at a price.'

This does represent a theme which runs continually through the essays in relation to lodgings, to sex, and to employment. No less than eight of the authors have made direct reference to colour tax. As part of a study of the degree of adaptation and integration achieved by African and Asian students at Oxford carried out by Dawson (1961), an analysis was made of the relative costs of accommodation for a group of 160 African and Asian men and women students as well as for a control group of 160 British students. It was found that African and Asian men paid 16s. a week more for lodgings than their British counterparts whilst women students paid 12s. a week more than the control group. It was also found that African and Asian students tended to live in lodging-houses of a semi-professional type close to the centre of Oxford, whilst the students from the control group tended to live with families in the more outlying suburbs. The differ-ences between the groups were statistically of high significance and confirmed the fact that African and Asian students were paying more and tending to live closer together. However, other variables had to be considered before interpretation in terms of 'colour tax' and dis-crimination could be put forward. For example, evidence was found that many of those students preferred to live together and tended to choose accommodation in which this was possible rather than isolate themselves. On the other hand, there was also considerable evidence that it was easier for African and Asian students to obtain this type of accommodation rather than the 'family' type.

All these difficulties related to lodgings create a sense of loneliness and frustration. Difficulties—real and imagined—in establishing relations with members of the opposite sex accentuate this still further. Eight of our writers seemed quite happy about this aspect of their lives. Of those, three were married to English girls, two were engaged to be married, and one had an English girl-friend. Seventeen students complained of minor difficulties in finding female companionship (refusals to dance and other similar sources of annoyance), while thirty went further and complained of the entire pattern of their relationship with native girls. The type of incidents and the specific nature of the complaints vary: e.g. relationships are only possible with foreign girls, neurotics, or semi-prostitutes; white girls who go out with coloured students are ostracized; parents forbid friendship with a coloured man; a minister of the Church told white girls not to go out with coloured men; a student was attacked by juveniles when out with a white girl, &c. On the whole, this is felt by our writers to be one of the salient aspects of the life of a coloured student in this country. 'Because of the strong emotions rooted in sexual matters', writes a Sudanese student, 'it would not be an exaggeration to say that racialism is deepest rooted here.' As one would expect, it is with respect to sex that sometimes the most painful or embarrassing experiences arise. 'To walk through the streets with a white girl at your side is to run the gauntlet of staring white faces—she could not possibly be decent.' Or, from another student: 'A university woman who forms a love relationship with a coloured man is quietly ostracized.' And another, referring to an English girl who contracted a mixed marriage: 'She is isolated from the rest of society . . . eyes fixed on her as if she had committed a crime.'

But even success in sexual matters may have its bitter ingredients. Some students feel that such success is sometimes not based on a decent human relationship but can be attributed to the legend of Negro sexual superiority. 'No frank discussion could omit a reference to the fact that even in Oxford it is strongly believed that a Negro is sexually superior. Whether or not this is a compliment, few Negroes can decide,' writes a West Indian. And so, writes another 'A West Indian can hardly be blamed for despising a woman who regards him as a foreign phallus.'

Carey interpreted much of this again in terms of a 'colour tax'. 'Because of their colour', he writes, 'these students are usually (only) able to contact women of a social standing and of an educational background below that acceptable to British students.' This statement is perhaps too sweeping. It could be argued that any male group, white or black, visiting another country on a temporary basis may have difficulty in forming normal relationships with women at equal socio-economic level. There is also some evidence from the essays that the degree of difficulty is related to cultural background and not to colour only. African students in the group apparently have most difficulty, Asian students are next, whilst West Indian students tend to have least difficulty—these differences are statistically highly significant. It is only here that the effect of country of origin on experience and adaptation becomes clearly apparent. The differences in terms of general patterns of prejudice and discrimination, or in terms of lodgings and employment, are not nearly so marked.

As many of the students live on grants that are not quite adequate, the experience of looking for jobs leads to a number of comments concerning discrimination in employment. The main theme running through these comments is the lack of jobs available to students which would be compatible with their qualifications. Of forty-six students who mentioned this issue, three only stated that they found no employment difficulties. Twelve referred to a considerable extent of discrimination, and thirty-one to some degree of it. There are reports that friendship shown by workers tends to be withdrawn when the student assumes a working role and the threatening characteristics of an economic competitor. A number of students pointed out that the main pressures in terms of economic competition were in the metropolitan areas such as London and Birmingham where there are the largest numbers of African, Asian, and West Indian workers. One student wrote that 'it is with the semi-skilled in the large industrial towns where the group pressures are sharpening. Economic insecurity where the supply of semi-skilled labour is abundant creates hostility towards the coloured group.'

Very few examples of academic discrimination are mentioned in the essays—a total of three, none of them of serious proportions. The following quotation from a West Indian is rather more typical of our students' reactions to the ups and downs of their academic career: 'It often works the other way; a Negro student who shows any promise is likely to be even more highly praised than a white one. This might be regarded as a form of patronage.' It is this quality of 'performer' which they think is attributed to them, the implication of delighted surprise in the praise bestowed on them, that seems to annoy some of the successful students among the writers of our essays. As this theme is treated at length in some of the essays contained in this collection, we shall not take space here to discuss it further.

*   *   *

Table 5 summarizes the various comments made on the role of the British Council and other organizations attempting to help in the students' adjustment in this country. As can be seen, the balance is quite favourable, particularly with regard to the British Council, though some comments are highly critical.

The role which organizations such as the British Council are playing in the immediate adjustment and general integration of students to life in Britain is considerable. There are some indications, however, that there is a need for more flexibility in the coping with different problems and expectations. There also appeared to be a need for organizations to provide these services without asking for too much information about life histories and without too many restrictions and controls.

TABLE 5*

ORGANIZATIONS IN BRITAIN

Nature of experience		Organizations and Experience	Number
Very helpful	17	British	10
		Rotary	2
		East and West Friendship	2
		Anti-Apartheid	1
		Y.M.C.A.	1
		Y.W.C.A.	1
Helpful	5	British Council	4
		Y.M.C.A.	1
Unhelpful	11	British Council	11

The provision of organized hospitality leads some students towards an ambivalent attitude, as they would obviously prefer to fit in within a normal network of less contrived human relationships. This is expressed, perhaps a little forcibly, in one of the essays published in this book: 'The British Council exists to provide organized kindness at 5s. a year. As such it satisfies felt needs. Because the organization supplies needs which in an integrated society would have found fulfilment in human relationships, it remains, like the accommodating woman, curiously unloved, even in use.'

THE IMAGE OF BRITAIN

There is no easy way to summarize the extraordinarily varied comments about Britain and the British that we found in the essays. It will be clear from the preceding pages that, on the whole, they are not likely to be enthusiastic. We came to the conclusion that the simplest way of conveying to the reader the general flavour of these comments was in the form of a quantitative summary, although we are keenly aware of the pitfalls of this type of pseudo-statistics: the small number of cases, the need to interpret comments which are sometimes ambiguous as favourable or unfavourable, the varying degree of intensity of the statements, &c. A summary of all these statements is set out in Table 6. The descriptive terms used by the authors were transcribed, as far as it was possible, to the headings which appear in the table. The assignment to categories 'favourable' or 'unfavourable' was made, in cases of doubt, on the basis of the context in which an evaluation appeared.

The general ratio of 5·3 unfavourable comments to 1 favourable is

*These data (and those in the subsequent tables) are based only on essays written by men.

a disturbing one, and it is unfortunately too striking to be ascribed to the lame statistics from which it emerges; it does obviously reflect the balance of opinion. In view of this high frequency of negative evaluations, the statements were analysed further from two points of view:

TABLE 6

COMMENTS BY STUDENTS ABOUT THE BRITISH

Favourable	Number	Unfavourable	Number
Friendly	6	Ignorant (this implies a lack of knowledge of coloured students and their countries)	25
Helpful	4		
Co-operative	3	Reserved	21
Polite	3	Patronizing	13
Courteous	3	Superior	10
Tolerant	2	'Conservative'	9
		Hypocritical	6
		Fear of neighbours' gossip	6
		Suspicious	4
		Condescending	4
		Sexual jealousy	3
		Insular	3
		Pity intead of friendship	3
		Curious	3
		Xenophobic	2
		Aloofness	2
		Self adoration	1
		Misunderstanding	1
		Self centred	2
		Coldness	1
Totals	21		119

their distribution in the three groups of students; and their distribution as function of the length of time spent in Britain.

Table 7 presents the pattern yielded by the breakdown according

TABLE 7

ANALYSIS OF ATTITUDES ACCORDING TO AREA OF ORIGIN AND TIME SPENT IN BRITAIN

Area of origin	Unfavourable	Ratio of number of comments to 1 student	Favourable	Ratio of number of comments to 1 student	Ratio: un-favourable to favourable
Africa (42)	75	1·79 : 1	10	0·24 : 1	7·5 : 1
Asia (16)	30	1·88 : 1	5	0·31 : 1	6·0 : 1
West Indians (10)	14	1·40 : 1	6	0·60 : 1	2·3: 1
Years spent in Britain					
0–1·9 (25)	35	1·40 : 1	6	0·24 : 1	5·8 : 1
2–3·9 (30)	57	1·90 : 1	10	0·33 : 1	5·7 : 1
4+ (13)	27	2·08 : 1	5	0·39 : 1	5·4 : 1

to the area of origin. Here again, the distribution is fairly clear-cut. The African ratio is the most unfavourable, followed by the Asian ratio, with the West Indian distribution far below the others in its relative frequency of unfavourable comment. This confirms the importance of similarity of cultural background in the adaptation to this country.

The same type of analysis was made with regard to the length of stay. As can be seen from Table 7 (lower half) the only slight trend that seems to emerge is an increased readiness to make comments, favourable or not, as function of the length of time spent here. There is a very slight tendency for the 'dislike ratio' to decrease with years, but it would be a bold man who would draw cheering conclusions from figures such as these. Unfortunately, the general conclusion of the preponderance of dislike is based on much clearer evidence.

CHANGES IN ATTITUDES

One cannot reach valid general conclusions about changes of attitudes from a collection of essays such as we received: the variety of form and content precludes any possibility of a systematic analysis. A good deal about these changes can be inferred from the previous description of experiences in Britain as they relate to expectations existing before arrival.

However, one conclusion can be reached based on the content analysis of the explicit statements found in the essays: that the number of those expressing satisfaction is lower than of those who held high expectations before arrival; and that the number of those whose final verdict is not favourable is higher than of those whose initial expectations were low.

But statements such as these are not very illuminating. They do not add anything to what has already been seen in the previous sections. A little more information is provided when a tally is made of the statements directly concerned with specific advantages and disadvantages in studying in Britain. Table 8 summarizes the content of these statements.

It can be seen from this table that the students are often aware of the hypersensitivity which arises from the general situation in which they find themselves. This type of reaction to real or imagined discrimination has been noted previously by P.E.P. (1955) and Carey (1956), and it does present a real problem. Judging from the themes running through the essays, this sharpened sensitivity leads to considerable difficulties of adjustment and sometimes it creates an unbridgeable gap between the student and the surrounding society. Here is one reaction of that nature extracted from an essay written by an Indian student:

At 17, I came over believing in my gifts, my ability to absorb, build, be assimilated by society here. . . . At 23, I find most British attempts at friendship disingenuous; think most jokes involving Negroes, darkies and wogs are tasteless; regard most failures to get a room as a deliberate slight, and whenever there's talk of British justice, law and order I pretend I'm not listening.

TABLE 8
ADVANTAGES AND DISADVANTAGES DERIVING FROM EDUCATION IN BRITAIN

Advantages	Number	Disadvantages	Number
Contact with British	18	Made to realize racial and colour differences	26
Made to identify with own national and racial group	13	Became hypersensitive	14
		Education of no value	1
Education	10	Difficulty in adjusting on return to one's own country	1
Contact with other nationalities	9	Became insecure	1
Total	50	Total	43

Two categories of statement listed in Table 8 are concerned with the sharper realization of racial and colour differences. More often than not this is placed in the context of a new awareness of race prejudice, although for many students the subsequent identification with their own national or racial groups stemming from this experience was considered to be new and enriching. This was particularly evident for West Indian students: 'In this atmosphere it is not strange that many West Indians give birth to Caribbean nationalism.' This same type of reaction concerning 'African-ness' or sometimes *négritude* was also mentioned by some African students.

*   *   *

The colour problem is the principal theme of the essays: it could not be otherwise, and not only because this is the central topic of the essay competition. This topic struck a chord because it related directly and intimately to something which is centrally important in the lives that the writers lead in this country.

A direct proof of this genuine preoccupation is the number of statements containing suggestions about 'what could be done', about ways and means to reduce prejudice and discrimination. We found no less than 147 such suggestions. Some of them do not go beyond a general statement of principle: more tolerance is needed in inter-group relations, more sympathy, efforts should be made to implement the United Nations Charter, &c. We thought, however, that a rough analysis of the more specific statements would be of some interest as a reflection of what is seen to be the source of the difficulties, and also as an expression of the attitudes towards the host society that emerged from all the difficulties and entanglements.

Table 9 sets out a categorization of those statements in which some specific suggestions were made.

TABLE 9
WHAT ACTION SHOULD BE TAKEN

Education

Education of public (no further specification)	41
Newspapers should give more balanced accounts of the countries concerned, and should not place so much emphasis on the 'primitive' nature of peoples and countries	8
Stop showing films of 'backward' Africa	7
Stop programmes on television such as 'Africa now'	7
Television and Press should help by providing accurate information	7
Stop the reinforcing of stereotypes (golliwogs, minstrels, &c.)	6
Libraries should have more up-to-date books on Africa	2
Ethical and moral instruction	1
Education of children to prevent the development of stereotypes; increase of contacts through mixed schooling	17
Exchange of students and teachers	1

Information before arrival in Britain

Explanation of problems and difficulties prior to arrival	15
Overseas organizations should explain British institutions more accurately	3
British Information Services should be more realistic	1

Church

The Church should take a firmer stand against prejudice	5

Legal action

There should be a law against discrimination	2

Mixed marriages

There should be more inter-marriage	2

The dominant opinion is that the British public needs to be educated. It must be education *for* tolerance, and it must also be prevention: something should be done to stop the dissemination of crude and misguided notions about foreign countries, particularly in Africa and in Asia.

There is considerable feeling against the type of film and television programme which emphasizes the primitive nature of the lands and peoples from which the students came. They point out that this type of programme does not present the developments which are taking place today—it only adds to the general ignorance about their countries. One Indian student comments: 'It seems ludicrous that the peoples of the East, the peoples of backward nations, of small nations, should train millions of young people in technologies and sciences originating in Britain and the young British remain so indifferent to them as people.'

Some students wrote of the inflexibility of stereotypes encountered in this country amongst the middle-aged. In contrast to this, many stressed the friendly attitude of the children, and some hoped that the solution to the problem could be found through the children. A Nigerian student wrote:

The average British youngster is most friendly, and has little inhibition when dealing with a foreigner. This is most vividly seen in schools and playgrounds when he plays freely with children from other parts of the world. But before he comes up to the grammar school level he has already been imbued with all sorts of notions about the 'other man'.

Opinions are also expressed that the Church is not making the most of its opportunities and fails to provide strong moral guidance with regard to problems of prejudice and discrimination. This is reflected in a series of comments such as: 'Britain is not a Christian country', 'Britain is a Christian country by name only', or 'It is . . . a pity that the tremendous influence of the various Christian Churches over the faithful has been inadequately used.'

It can also be seen from the tables that the plea for adequate information before arrival, already discussed in one of the previous sections, is again made in this context by quite a number of students. There is no doubt that this is one of the clear-cut and consistent themes in the essays.

*   *   *

The picture we had to present is not encouraging, and it is part of a larger and even less encouraging pattern. Race prejudice in one form or another appears all over the world, and it is primarily a psychological problem. Acts of discrimination must be considered in relation to their background of prejudice, but they must also be seen in the light of economic, social, political, and historical conditions; there can be no easy 'solutions', no simple plans of action. The problems are difficult and they are deeply rooted in the structure of our society and of the societies from which the students come.

But it is possible that something could be done more or less immediately. Some of the problems discussed in the essays could be dealt with to some extent at an institutional level. There are many institutions directly or indirectly concerned with Commonwealth and foreign students in this country, and the responsibility for action should be laid squarely at their doorsteps. Universities and colleges, student bodies, Government departments and agencies, voluntary organizations, &c., have not sufficiently co-ordinated their efforts and have not devised a coherent programme. It is true that even if such a programme existed and was implemented one could still not hope that drastic improvements would take place. But the problem is sufficiently important to warrant an attempt, even if only moderate success can be expected. The choice is between initiating some form of action on a limited scale or waiting until—miraculously—prejudice and discrimination disappear from our social scene.

REFERENCES

British Council, *Overseas Students in Britain*, London, 1962.

Carey, A. T., *Colonial Students*, Secker & Warburg, London, 1956.

Dawson, J. L. M., 'An Analysis of the Degree of Adaptation achieved by Oxford University African and Asian Students', Paper read to J.A.C.A.R.I., 1961.

Political and Economic Planning, *Colonial students in Britain*, P.E.P., London, 1955.

Singh, K. A., *Indian Students in Britain*, Asia Publishing House, New York, 1963.